RULES
FOR
MODERN
LIFE

SIR DAVID TANG

PORTFOLIO
PENGUIN

For the precious sextet in my life:
Mother, Lucy, Victoria, Edward, Minnie and Naughtins

PORTFOLIO PENGUIN

UK | USA | Canada | Ireland | Australia
India | New Zealand | South Africa

Portfolio Penguin is part of the Penguin Random House group of companies
whose addresses can be found at global.penguinrandomhouse.com.

First published 2016

001

Copyright © The Financial Times Limited, 2016

Illustrations by Tom Jennings, www.tomjennings.me

The moral right of the author has been asserted

Set in 11/13 pt Dante MT Std
Typeset by Jouve (UK), Milton Keynes
Printed in Great Britain by Clays Ltd, St Ives plc

A CIP catalogue record for this book is available from the British Library

ISBN: 978–0–241–25851–4

www.greenpenguin.co.uk

Penguin Random House is committed to a
sustainable future for our business, our readers
and our planet. This book is made from Forest
Stewardship Council® certified paper.

RULES FOR MODERN LIFE

'Incisive, outrageous and preposterously entertaining. Reading these essays in style, manners, gossip, grace and good sense is like sharing a private railway carriage with a mad but marvellous maharajah. I never wanted the journey to end' **Stephen Fry**

'Funny, clever and disgraceful. In terms of a useful guide to modern living, it knocks the New Testament into a cocked hat' **Richard Curtis**

'David Tang is the second funniest David in the world' **David Walliams**

'Excellent advice that we didn't know we needed' **Sir Michael Caine**

'I absolutely love *Rules for Modern Life*! David's amazing sense of humour and wit keep one glued to this 'pop culture bible' that everyone MUST read. It is not only educational but enlightening as well. Bravo David!' **Tommy Hilfiger**

'David Tang always brings something extra to life, which is what we all want' **Sir Mick Jagger**

'Uncompromising and full of style. You will laugh out loud' **Tracey Emin**

'David Tang is effortless in his sense of style and being. And that's how it should be' **Naomi Campbell**

'I feel a curious joy of life when I am around David Tang. He knows best' **Eva Herzigova**

'Sharply funny and surprisingly informative. I would rather read style notes from the pen of Tang than any other source on the planet' **Joanna Lumley**

'A marvellous compendium of good manners and good sense in society, reinforced with insight and sly humour' **Wilbur Smith**

'Filled with valuable advice. Amusingly written and a real pleasure to read' **Sir Terence Conran**

'I have long admired David's irrepressible humour, quick wit and keen eye for style. This anthology is a collection of indispensable wisdom' **Lord Foster**

'Eloquent and humorous' **Eric Schmidt**

'A degree course in 21st-century decorum. It will make an aristocrat out of an arriviste' **Duke of Marlborough**

'David is a life-changer' **Mario Testino**

'Hilarious and edifying. Absolutely essential reading about the nuances as well as the complexities of life today' **Dame Julia Peyton-Jones**

'David Tang is the thinking woman's Fu Manchu. If you are allergic to the combination of wit, brains and mischief you won't enjoy this book' **Barry Humphries**

'David Tang is an astute observer of the social scene with a wicked sense of humour. A most welcome read in these dark times' **Adrian Zecha**

'Anyone who wants to move up the social ladder, or avoid sliding down, must read *Rules for Modern Life*. It is the essential primer for 21st-century social success' **Geordie Greig**

'A perfect compendium of distinguished, humorous and polished advice for a gentlemanly way of living' **Leonardo Ferragamo**

'Wise, witty and wicked, with useful advice for living' **Anouska Hempel**

'David Tang is the most provocative, amusing, sophisticated, counter-intuitive and energetic man I know, and these qualities are present on every single page of this remarkable anthology' **Nicholas Coleridge**

'Genuinely hilarious' **Robin Birley**

'David Tang is a living treasure and a unique polymath' **Nicolas Berggruen**

David Tang is my 'UNCLE DAVE':

Unique
Notorious
Charismatic
Lovable
Eccentric
Daring
Anal
Vivacious
Enigmatic

Kate Moss

CONTENTS

• • •

• • •

DAVID TANG'S little section used to be interesting, but it has deteriorated into a selection of self-serving questions aimed to elevate his social standing and reputation. It has become a bore regardless of how hard he tries to convince readers otherwise. He should be replaced by someone more genuine and interesting. This suggestion should be taken constructively by him, and is not meant as an insult. One who cannot take honest criticism should spend more time with sycophants.

If you think that I am doing this column in order to enhance my social standing and reputation, and that I would become more famous and a better networker, would climb up the social ladder and command greater celebrity status; and that by being a regular contributor to the *FT*, the most prestigious international paper in the world, I would become the envy of other writers, established or aspiring – then you would be absolutely correct.

SARTORIAL ADVICE

*'Why would any real man wish to wear
a butterfly round his collar?'*

I ENJOY DISPENSING SARTORIAL advice because I have always been interested in the gradual shifts and changes in society in which fashion figures centrally. Besides, I was heavily involved in a retail business that thrives on fashion. So I have always made a conscious effort to educate myself in its history and evolution, not only in the mainstream West, but also in the peripheral East. Western fashion moves very quickly, in fact by the season, and so it is important to be consciously contemporary in order to be authoritative. This constantly changing landscape means there is always a plethora of opinions to consider, but essentially my advice would be to opt for the sensibilities of US *Vogue* under the laser sensor of Anna Wintour. Her thermometer is mercury sharp, and others disagree with her at their peril.

Fashion in the East moves much more slowly. For example, the djellaba and the burka have not changed at all as the years have gone by, and the Arab wardrobe today might well be identical to that of the time of Lawrence of Arabia. Indeed, the biggest changes of fashion in the past 50 years in the East – from the Middle East and across Central Asia to East Asia and even Japan – have come from the West. This infiltration is manifested through two items: gym shoes or trainers; and jeans. Trainers are now the universal footwear, whether in the city, town, desert, mountains or forest. They are worn alike by steady urban dwellers and precarious refugees running away from conflicts. Jeans have also become one of the most worn items in the world. The only question for the cognoscenti is whether the ripped versions invented in the West will now spread to the East, where people expect their clothes to last, and not deliberately have them torn across the knees and the lower cheeks of the posterior.

Sartorial advice is led by icons, too. Coco Chanel banged on about simplicity as beauty and was renowned for her unfussy colours, cuts and patterns. She also put women in men's clothes, creating the androgynous look. In turn, Yves Saint Laurent was credited with putting women in trousers – although Chairman Mao did that before him in China, but possibly with a lesser sense of fashion, and certainly of the crease. Now, today's far-reaching social media helps fashion voyeurs to see what their contemporary style icons are wearing, from the Beckhams to Kate Moss, or from Kanye West to, at the other end of the spectrum, the Duke of Edinburgh. The reason why they lead is because of their sense of confidence: the confidence of mix and match, the confidence of believing that what they wear looks best on them, and the confidence of not really caring what other people think.

Mind you, some people end up with too much confidence. I am thinking of Liberace and Karl Lagerfeld and Kim Jong-un and Fidel Castro, for example, and their signature attires. The dress sense of these extraordinary people is immediately recognizable. I only wish someone had had the guts to tell them that what they were wearing was a bit over the top. I once had lunch in a tent in the Sahara with Colonel Gaddafi. He was in full uniform, with enough medals to decorate the Spartans at Thermopylae. The tassels from his epaulettes would not have looked out of place on Barbara Cartland's drawing-room curtains, and I certainly didn't dare ask who his barber was, as his hair dangled down like a tangle of seaweed, still less his facial beautician, as his cheeks looked like the surface of the moon. Another dictator, Robert Mugabe, once came to my house for lunch in the height of summer in Hong Kong. It was 33 degrees C with 98 per cent humidity. He arrived in a tie and a three-piece suit. I implored him to disrobe, perhaps not so much because we were going to be eating in the garden, which was very hot and humid, but

4

because his tailor must have been blind, and I didn't want the president lunching as a scarecrow.

There are, however, those who care a great deal about how they look. I was once on a boat anchored adjacent to another one belonging to a very good friend of mine who had P. Diddy, or Puff Daddy, staying on board. We all went ashore for dinner, and afterwards were about to troop off to a club for a nightcap when P. Diddy said he wanted to return to the boat first. I was rather curious why the rap star wanted to do that, as it involved getting into a tender and going out to the anchor before coming back again. His host was able to enlighten me that P. Diddy always wanted a change of clothes upon a change of venue. Not only that, he was given an extra cabin on the boat in which an ironing board with a valet was on permanent standby to facilitate these changes. P. Diddy, incidentally, was already dressed meticulously in an immaculate white suit with a silk cravat and his signature dark shades. Anyway, he came to the nightclub after about an hour, in a gleaming black suit and another silk scarf, which had obviously been pressed very shortly before.

In any case, the internet age has led to the traditional manifestation of wealth through clothes being superseded by 'geek chic'. Steve Jobs was one of the most visible proponents of this form of attire, in his jeans and pumps. So too were Bill Gates and other cyber billionaires such as Mark Zuckerberg, with the result that formal wear is no longer de rigueur among those for whom the internet has brought fame and fortune. But I am not sure I like this trend of dressing down. A dress code shows respect to others. I also believe strongly that society as a whole looks so much better when people take the trouble to dress properly. It's a rite that has done well for mankind. Confucius, who wrote his *Book of Rites* 2,500 years ago, encouraged people to respect formality as a good way of living. So I hope the pendulum might swing back the other way, and that those who can afford it take trouble over sartorial guidelines. Just remember Cary Grant or Stewart

Granger, or even Edward G. Robinson in his roles as a gangster: they all wore beautifully tailored suits and they looked incredibly smart. The same with Sophia Loren or Ingrid Bergman: they always looked resplendent in their dresses. And that is the joy of fashion: though it might sometimes be regarded as superficial, it has nonetheless been very effective in creating an endless kaleidoscope of visual feasts, not only on celluloid, but also in reality, which is living art.

ACCESSORIES

If unmarried, which is the proper hand on which to wear a signet ring? In what direction should the initials be facing – towards the wearer, or away? Same with initialled cufflinks – towards the wearer, or away?

The signet ring, which has always been the symbol of the Sloane Ranger or the British upper-class twit, should always be worn on the last finger of the left hand. But snobbery dictates that it is one's family crest and not initials that should be inscribed on it. If you have no family crest, you shouldn't really be wearing a signet ring. If tortured for advice, I suppose the crest should face oneself, as it should be worn for pride and not for flaunting.

Is wearing cufflinks on a single cuff shirt a complete sartorial no-no?

Not at all. Double cuffs are only de rigueur on dress shirts. I have many shirts with single cuffs made by Charvet, the best shirt-maker in the world. In the company's bespoke room above its shop overlooking the Place Vendôme in Paris, Mademoiselle Anne-Marie Colban, daughter of the owner, is able to offer

104 shades of white. If she can make shirts with single cuffs for cufflinks, I'd be foolish to worry about any sartorial faux pas.

Wristwatch – battery, automatic, manual wind, or none? Or pocket watch instead?

Nobody carries pocket watches any more. For those who do, they are usually pompous types who want to show off their gold or silver chain. However, I am prepared to make an exception of Hercule Poirot.

What would be your personal choice for a formal and everyday watch?

I always prefer a thin watch to a thick one, if only because I want to wear it comfortably under my cuffs. The great Gianni Agnelli, who owned Fiat and was probably as stylish a man as Coco Chanel was a stylish woman, always wore his watches over his cuffs, which eliminated the use of cufflinks, which I rather like. Nowadays, the fad is for watches to be obese, not unlike most of the Russians and Arabs and Eurotrash who are invariably seen to sport these huge chunks of watch.

I also bemoan the disappearance of the fluorescent watches that use radioactive sources. In these days of pathetic health and safety, the mere suggestion of radioactivity would send regulating busybodies spinning, even though the amount employed was always infinitesimal. But, thankfully, the use of gas has managed to replace the radioactive method, and there is now a handful of watches which indeed fluoresce brightly in the dark.

But one must be careful about such efficient illumination. A friend of mine once woke up in the middle of the night, looked at his brightly lit dial and shouted out alarmingly: 'Oh my God,

I have got to go, I have to get home, it's so late.' Then a familiar voice was heard to say: 'Darling, you ARE home.'

Wallet – in hip or breast pocket?

A wallet in a hip pocket will make your trousers look odd because hips on trousers are usually fairly tight, and therefore putting anything in them will create unattractive bulges or strange-looking contour lines.

I wonder if you can advise me on the best article in which to carry one's spectacles, cigarettes and lip gloss when staying at large country houses, rather than to lumber around with my Fendi handbag from room to room, which seems rather Miss Marpleish and deeply middle class.

A minor member of the British royal family once observed to me that the best way to conceal one's spectacles/cigarettes/lipstick is to shove them all into a pair of gloves which one would casually carry, but not wear, in one hand. Placing this pair of gloves on the table, which by itself suggests a sense of occasion, especially if they were made from understated embroidered black silk, would look very chic, doubly so with the dispensation of any bourgeois bag.

What about briefcases/attaché cases? Or are you so elevated that some underling carries the briefcase that contains the fat enamelled fountain pen with which you sign deals with flourish and elan?

This might well be your fantasy but it is not my reality. I do use a fountain pen, but it is thin and made of plastic by Pelikan, which produces nibs so smooth they glide across even lavatory paper. The only enamel I come into contact with is when, after a hard day's work, I slide into a nice hot bath, resting my nape on this magical paint half-in and half-out of the water, feeling that unique sensation of equilibrium between the heat of the water and the coolness of the coated cast-iron bathtub.

I do not carry briefcases or attaché cases, because I am not a civil servant, and when travelling I prefer a shoulder bag slung across the opposing shoulder. The only time I might dream of having a lackey is whenever I arrive at Gatwick airport, which is too mean to provide any free trolleys at its departure terminal. Neither are there any porters to speak of, unlike every airport in the US. Instead, passengers are expected to lug their own loads and walk a fair distance up an incline before entering the building. As none of my old-fashioned suitcases are fitted with wheels, I end up checking in looking like a gorilla with arms stretched long by weights.

NECKWEAR

For someone so opinionated on style, why, in your byline photo, are the handkerchief in your pocket and your tie of the same material? I always thought that this was a real no-no.

In all my life, I have never worn a tie and a pocket handkerchief of the same material. Of course it's a no-no. But then you are too clever by half by suggesting that I have done so. If you were to look closely, my tie came from Voyage, the shop that refused entry to Madonna and eventually went bankrupt; and my pocket handkerchief came from Etro, from one of its ladies' scarves which I cut in half. I must give you the name of my oculist.

What is your view on bow ties? They seem to be well regarded in the US but not much in evidence in Europe.

Bow ties look ridiculous, unless you are either Bob Hope or Robin Day, who looked ridiculous – the former with a hockey-stick chin, and the latter with Bavarian eyebrows. Bow ties are also rather effeminate, as they look exactly like a butterfly. Why would any real man wish to wear a butterfly round his collar?

I am responding to your disdain for men wearing a bow tie. I am reading the August copy of *Vanity Fair* magazine and there you are in Robin Birley's Loulou's nightclub, resplendent in a beautiful bow tie. Since you say that bow ties are de rigueur with clowns, you now complement the trio of Groucho Marx, Jerry Lewis and Pee-wee Herman.

I was, you fool, in my black tie, which is an evening ensemble with a black bow tie as a constituent part – totally different from a single non-black bow tie worn in the day with anything you like.

Here's a new poser for you. I was told by my late Edwardian-era uncle that it is incorrect to wear a tie plus a breast-pocket handkerchief, 'an unfortunate habit affected by cads and well-dressed savages'. He proclaimed that a handkerchief in the top pocket is acceptable with a sports jacket or blazer with open-neck shirt. The real art, sadly forgotten by me, is wearing a hanky up your sleeve; pulling the handkerchief out with a flourish to mop up a spill or tearful dinner partner. You may be the only person who knows the trick of keeping the aforesaid linen or silk up the sleeve so it's available but won't, in the normal course of events, fall out.

You cannot nowadays go round tucking your handkerchief up your sleeve as if you were Oscar Wilde. It is a fashionable affectation well past its sell-by date. It's like wearing a cravat with an open-neck shirt or having a saw-tooth pocket handkerchief without being the Duke of Edinburgh. As for your Edwardian uncle, he might have been more correct to observe that a tie and a breast-pocket handkerchief should never match. There are those who put on matching sets whom I imagine pull the handkerchief out of their breast pocket only to find its end attached to the tie! Study the Prince of Wales. He always wears a tie plus a breast-pocket handkerchief, but of course always different and never matching! Would your pompous uncle have called him a cad or a savage? I rather think not.

Can you tell me the best way to store neck ties?

Not rolled up à la small bundles of hay and stuffed tightly into a drawer – if only because you then can't see the tie properly, and when one is extracted the whole lot collapses, with the inevitable bother of having to roll them like sushi back into order. Hang them, for God's sake!

Do you ever wear a cravat?

Egad, no! Certainly not since Yves Saint Laurent died.

I would not expect you to wear a cravat, but what are your views on the custom among men to wear suits without a tie? Once the preserve of hedge-fund managers circling Berkeley Square or members of the Israeli Knesset (at least

they have the excuse of sweltering heat), it seems that most men have now succumbed to this trend.

It started with the yuppies, who regarded themselves as smooth enough to shed the standard City dress code of suit and tie. Next came the internet geeks who wanted to copy the likes of Steve Jobs and Bill Gates by ditching ties and wearing jeans. So now it is acceptable to go round, and even be admitted to a snooty nightclub, in an open-neck shirt without a tie. For the Israeli Knesset, or other parliaments in hot places, you are right that heat is the main reason why their members don't wear ties. In the case of Greece, it might be because none of them can afford one lately and are really feeling the heat under their collars.

DRESSING FOR HOT WEATHER

Is it ever permissible for a gentleman to wear sandals or even flip-flops? What footwear can one don during hot weather and still retain one's dignity?

When Jock Delves Broughton shot himself in the heat of Africa, he did it in a three-piece linen suit because he was a real gent, suffering a wife who was blatantly unfaithful to him. Imagine asking him to wear sandals or flip-flops. Perish the thought!

Certainly, in his generation, particularly during the days of the Raj, everyone dressed immaculately in layers, in steaming conditions in that subcontinent. And they all looked pretty dignified to me. Yet we have all become rather sloppy in our dress sense, mistaking casualness for comfort, and conflating comfort with elegance. I just can't help thinking how elegantly people dressed in the old days. They must think that we are now all pansies, demanding air-conditioning everywhere – and, worse, slobs who shuffle around in open shoes.

I am writing to ask what you think of white suits. I am undecided as to whether they are acceptable or beyond the pale. Naff or natty? Before I commission my tailor to make one, I thought that I should discover whether or not one forms part of your wardrobe.

White-white is not on. Off-white begins to be acceptable but there are really two antecedents for an off-white suit to be acceptable: first, it has to be in linen, and linen that is lined so that it does not crumple easily and become Berlusconian. Second, it should not be a suit – in other words, the shade of the off-white should be slightly different between the jacket and the trousers. You will notice that the Prince of Wales gets it spot on whenever he sports what might appear to be a white suit, but on closer examination, it's really a pair of off-white trousers and a slightly different shade of off-white jacket. For maximum effect, both pieces of garment should be used and old, but immaculately and freshly pressed. Needless to say, the trousers should have turn-ups of 1¼ inches, and the bottom no wider than 17¼ inches, and never have a break on the trousers, so as to be cool in a climate for which a white suit is required.

While cruising through Tuscany's vineyards as a wine journalist, I could not help pondering about a proper though temporary place for sunglasses in short moments of sun-absence. Should I hold them, which I find inconvenient and slightly annoying, or should I hang them

on the upper button of my shirt, which I consider not-viewy? Thank you.

Learn from Karl Lagerfeld how and why he keeps his sunglasses on even in the darkest eclipses. But I suspect his propensities are different from yours, and since yours clearly lean towards the vino, your best solution is to act like a sommelier. So dangle your sunglasses at the end of a chain round your neck. I know this might look a bit old-fashioned. On the other hand if you were to carry the *tastevin* as well as your sunglasses, you would be able to boast about the practical ingenuity of killing two birds with one stone. And if you were to be dramatic, you might even add to the chain a small napkin with which to do your wiping of both. But try not to clash the colour of your napkin with your shirt.

Not long ago, Tom Ford remarked that shorts are not for gentlemen (or something along those lines). Do you wear shorts?

Of course I wear shorts when I am on holiday on a beach, around the pool, on the deck of a boat or walking in the heat, none of which has anything to do with being a gentleman or not, but being practical and sensible. What Tom Ford might be referring to is the wearing of shorts in town, which indeed is unacceptable, if only because most of us have rather unsavoury hairy shins. They are usually a shocking sight. In Hong Kong, where I have a private club, I had to send out warnings to members not to wear shorts, even in the tropical heat, because men who choose to wear them seldom, if ever, have a shapely physique. But of course I would make an exception for the likes of David Beckham, who would look perfect coming into the club in his shorts as a mega-football star. How amusing would that be! If he did so, I am sure all of us would burst into spontaneous applause. So there are occasions when even Tom Ford could be wrong.

Advice please on what colour shirt to wear in a hot climate (or a tight corner). I love blue shirts, but they do tend to show perspiration.

From a scientific point of view, white for a hot climate because it reflects heat. Any darker shade will absorb heat. Ergo, common sense dictates the lightest colour that also camouflages sweat. Certainly, no patterned shirts, particularly floral ones à la Hawaiian short sleeves. They are unacceptable at all times except for Jack Lord when he was alive.

What are your views on linen as a summer fabric?

I like the thought of wearing linen but abhor the reality. Linen garments tend to crease the moment you put them on. Crumpled linens always remind me either of all those majors with moustaches in the days of the Raj, or modern Eurotrash self-conscious about their Armani jackets. I can tolerate the former because their linens were invariably multi-ply and therefore less creased, and in their three-piece suits they stand for that stiff upper-lip spirit of ignoring the tropical heat and humidity for the sake of sartorial propriety. And there is something romantic about linens in the tropics. Creased-up linen sheets inside mosquito nets in Kenya, say, evoke for me the languid allure of a beautiful and young Greta Scacchi as the mistress of *White Mischief*, replete with forbidden romance and illicit mystery. So for me, I wouldn't mind linen sheets with which to improve my dreams.

The Eurotrash, however, usually contrive to accentuate the

crumpledness of their single-ply linen but end up looking any-thing but smooth, which is how they want to look. The Japanese designer Issey Miyake went further and constructed deliberately crumpled clothes with permanent accordion creases for those who don't mind walking round like failed pieces of human origami. His clothes are also made to be screwed up into small balls or rolls for ease of packing, the ingenuity of which German *Fräuleins* or Americans with plastic surgery are keen to brag about and demonstrate, often with tedium.

Is it OK to go sockless when wearing a suit?

It is highly unpleasant to look at any sockless person, especially with a suit because it would highlight their naked ankles and possibly hair around the bottom of the shin. Both of these are as 'no-no' as Nanette! In any case, isn't the prospect of sweating in a pair of leather shoes altogether rather unsavoury? It doesn't take a great deal of imagination to smell the consequences.

SPECIAL OCCASIONS

Is black tie for funerals?

Yes, if you mean wearing a tie that is black. But not 'black tie' as an ensemble, which nowadays is regarded as formal wear, usually with ghastly bows already knotted, irregular lapels, dubious waist-coats and unacceptable colour handkerchiefs over the top pocket.

Whenever I go to an open event like the Chelsea Flower Show, I am in a state of menopausal anxiety about my outfit. How can I make sure that I get it right?

If you are not famous, nobody will care. Anyway, it's much more chic at the Chelsea Flower Show to appear in proper old and worn country wear, rather than a smart frock and a hat. Women overdressed, over-made-up and over-heeled should be arrested.

Recently, I was invited to be the best man at my brother's wedding. I was told I had to wear a vest, but decided those who wear vests are better at serving drinks. So I decided on a cummerbund. I also ditched the studs and cufflinks. The bride was not happy. Thoughts?

My thoughts are that you should know it is the ridiculous and cumbersome cummerbund that would have made you look like a waiter. The vest you mention is called a waistcoat, and at a wedding you would never wear a black one.

Instead, as for Royal Ascot, the waistcoat is de rigueur, often in light colours and smartest with contrasting piping. Studs? I hope you are referring to the stiff collar for which studs are required. So if you dispensed with them, you must have been in a limp collar. Cufflinks: one must have cufflinks on a pair of double cuffs for a formal occasion. No wonder it was not a good day for you. If you had been better informed and dressed, your sister-in-law might have been less displeased.

The wedding party starts at 6.30pm, black tie. Should ladies wear long or short? I think long but advice is needed. Short would be longer than knee-length.

When I founded and ran the fashion chain Shanghai Tang for seven years, I stupidly forgot to design a long dress that would transform itself into a short one, either by way of the bottom being lifted to the top or somehow camouflaged, or torn off altogether. Such a dress, if done properly, would solve a lot of problems for women who seem to fret endlessly about long and short. It would save so much email space and telephone time in our increasingly vacuous world if women did not have to ring each other about what they wear. Unless you are incredibly famous and expect to be photographed all the time, and publicity is part of your livelihood, it makes no sense for mortals to over-fuss about how they dress. In the evenings, hardly anyone pays much attention to anything from the waist down. I would love it to be standard practice for women to come without any make-up or high heels, so that we can see them au naturel. Dressing up is designed to make women look prettier than they are, which is a deception; worse still, with a plethora of plastic surgery. I once shared a lift with a well-known socialite whose facial deception was rather alarming. I thought I was in a BMW wind tunnel.

Where have you been? My run of lifetime luck continues as I get to meet the Potus. Please help! I don't know what to wear. I am only advised black tie is not required. Your wise counsel would be, as always, sincerely appreciated.

You would need to elaborate on the circumstances of your rendezvous. There is 'meeting the Potus' and there is 'meeting the Potus'. If you are going to be in a reception of an ocean of people and might only get the chance to shake his hand, and perhaps pressing and not letting go his flesh long enough for a desperate snap, then I'd say it wouldn't matter what you wear. Nobody would notice or give a hoot. At these largish receptions, you would be wise not to wear black tie lest you be mistaken for a waiter. If, however, you are going to a small gathering or a fairly intimate repast (of no more than a dozen, say), then it would be perfectly in order to telephone the presidential social secretary at the White House for the exact dress code: not to ascertain what you are not required to wear, but what you are asked to wear. You would look a bit old-fashioned if you turned up in cowboy boots and a lasso if dinner were in one of the state-rooms; or in full military uniform with miniatures while the Potus turns up in shirtsleeves and slacks and sneakers for relaxed al fresco dining.

Whenever in doubt, I would choose an ethnic garment such as a tailored Mao jacket which would pass cunningly as either formal (all buttoned up) or casual (unbuttoned). Such ethnicity also adds a touch of sophistication. But this could sometimes be turned into overkill if you were to be some incautious African chief, say. I have seen 'fanfare' attire that is more reminiscent of Eddie Murphy in *Coming to America* than any sartorial elegance. In the case of Barack Obama, he might even think, if you settled for flowing African tribal gear with rings jammed round your earlobes, that you were taking the mickey out of him.

When is it appropriate to wear ethnic garb – Scottish kilt, Chinese silk gown, Bavarian Lederhosen, etc. – outside one's home country?

It all depends whether you wish to bring attention upon yourself. You can certainly do that by dressing up, and you don't need to go ethnic.

I remember the Duchess of York arriving at an event in a dress so incandescent, enormous and crumpled that she might have been mistaken for a work of art by Christo – or even for Frank Gehry's Guggenheim Museum in Bilbao.

That was a paradigm of how you don't need to be in any ethnic mode and yet become the centre of attention. I often wear my Chinese silk or velvet outfit at black-tie dinners, and nobody fusses. But a couple of exceptions: a ninja tight-fitting suit or a flowing burka would stick out like sore thumbs.

IN THE COUNTRYSIDE

I am in mild need of a new shooting suit but am hesitant in going to many obvious choices because of a reluctance to get threads similar to everyone else. You have a smart grey suit that I recall admiring. Where would you recommend? I imagine you to be the definitive expert on something so subtle and important.

A new shooting suit is an open invitation to be mobbed up by others. Much smarter for your suit to be threadbare than for you to have new threads. Indeed, you will always find good shots in well-worn suits, often with noticeable darning or patches that *nouveaux* brands such as Dunhill put on to new jackets *ab initio*, which is exceedingly common. In any event, a gun would always wear an old Barbour over the suit. So why bother with a new suit? It is dangerous to dress too smartly at a shoot when you can't shoot properly. It's infinitely better to be a crack shot in shabby clothes than to be a crap shot in fancy gear.

At a famous shoot, one of my fellow guests, known for his sartorial eccentricity, insisted that the only acceptable footwear for such an occasion was black brogues, citing as his authority one of our leading dukes. Thus clad, and despite clear advice to the contrary, he was forced to wade up to his calves through a freezing torrent of water. Should we admire his steadfast refusal to abandon his high standards; or should we ridicule his gesture as vainglorious foppery?

There are two types of pretentiousness: one calculated to attract attention even if it involves discomfiture; and the second, through genuine eccentricity without regard to comfort. The question is, therefore, one of intention. I have a couple of friends who traipse over the grouse moors in their brogues: the first a City banker showing off his ostensible macho attitude, and the second a mad Scotsman who is used to walking all over his estate in ordinary shoes. What gives the game away is that the former has brown brogues (incorrect), while the latter has black ones (correct).

I recently purchased a pair of Swims from Norway. Is it proper to wear galoshes or improper? Having my feet dry is a luxury up there with having heat. However, there are a lot of people who abhor the very sight of galoshes covering up their luxury badges!

There is nothing wrong with galoshes even though I find anything entirely rubbery and used as a sheath unnatural and off-putting. Just think of surgical gloves! Horrible. I don't wear galoshes mainly because I believe that a well-made pair of shoes should be able to cope with wetness in nature and if its leather cracks, then that's good old natural wrinkles. It will be a sad day indeed if we have to start worrying about the equivalent of plastic surgery for shoes!

SHOES – BROWN OR BLACK?

I was rather surprised to observe on television recently a young presenter dressed in a very smart dark suit but wearing a pair of brown shoes. This was followed by two other presenters, again in dark suits sporting brown shoes.

I was under the impression that such a combination was very taboo. Perhaps I am out of touch. I would very much welcome your views please.

I really don't think you should fret over the colour of shoes worn by others! It is true that, for the English, brown shoes are rather frowned upon. For the consummate snob, even at a shoot, black shoes rather than brown shoes should be worn, and certainly no Englishman would ever wear brown shoes during the week in the city. But just remember what Deng Xiaoping said: 'It doesn't matter about the colour of the cat as long as it catches mice.' So my view is that it doesn't matter about the colour of the shoes as long as they are good for walking in. I once bribed my way to the papal cobbler in Rome, who made me a couple of pairs of shoes similar to those worn by the Pope – in orange and yellow. They are absolutely splendid. But I have yet to wear them on television.

While, unlike a certain footballer, I would never wear brown shoes with a blue or grey suit, I believe that in a more casual context brown shoes may be worn with blue jeans. The question that results is what colour socks should I wear? Not being Italian, no socks is not an option.

If you wear brown shoes with blue jeans, you are already three-quarters of the way to looking dodgy. Wear no socks, and you will indeed look like an Italian with big emotions – or typical Eurotrash. Wear dark-coloured socks, and you will look awkward by trying to appear smooth and failing to do so. Light-coloured socks, and you will look effeminate. Coloured or patterned socks, and you will look like a contrived Sloane. My advice is not to wear blue jeans with brown shoes at all.

Last week your discussion about brown shoes made me inquisitive. Since I am not familiar with the British etiquette for wearing them, could you please enlighten me: under which circumstances and with what outfit is it proper to wear them? I am ready to dispose of my brown shoes by Rossetti, Berluti, Loewe, and am prepared to purchase a few pairs of black shoes by John Lobb.

If you don't care about the British toffs, then wear your brown shoes even to a wedding. But if you like to emulate them, then remember toffs wear black shoes during the week, and brown shoes only in the country, particularly during the shooting season from the 'Glorious Twelfth' (August) to 1 February. Many brown shoes and boots will be found treading on heather, in butts and mud, and on hills and fields. So you don't have to chuck away any of your brown shoes if you were to wear them for shooting, hunting, fishing, farming or gardening, merging the brown colour into nature, which is why they are worn by gents.

Please don't drop a name like John Lobb, because you ought to refer to that famous cobbler as 'Lobbs'. More importantly, distinguish Lobbs owned by Hermès, which produces ready-made pairs, and Lobbs in London, which only does bespoke. Your throw-away remark about purchasing 'a few pairs of black shoes by John Lobb' will be exposed by the cognoscenti, as even with an old customer like myself, and I have been using them for almost 40 years, the last pair of shooting boots I had made took 11 months. Lobbs bespoke never rushes.

Frenchmen love wearing brown shoes, probably to upset the Brits. I hope they carry on, because virtually all of the world's most vulgar *nouveaux riches* from Central Asia, the Middle East and Russia are swanking around places like London and Paris in brown shoes, quite a few with the nasty version of the pointed design resembling stilettos or a Flamenco dancer. This will make the French extremely common. When in France, I make a point of staring at their brown shoes and then catching their eyes by saying '*Zdravstvuyte*', which never fails to annoy them.

Italians also wear brown shoes often even with blue suits. And they can pull off the trick.

I have received a great deal of mail about brown shoes. Having had many more discussions with my friends, I might have to revise my answer. First, I now accept that there are still gentlemen who go around in brown shoes and blue suits in town on weekdays. Furthermore, to be an uber-snob, one should always shoot in black shoes. Lord Sefton and Sir Eric Penn have been staunch proponents of this snobbery. Ergo, the Italians might not be as trendy as they think.

AGE-APPROPRIATE

Do you think parents should advise or even control how their teenage children dress?

'Yes' is the general answer: but not because the parents are paying, directly or indirectly, for all the clothes, and therefore they think they can legislate on what should be worn, but because it is lazy parenting when teenage children are left to dress exactly how they like to, and lazy parenting results in children acquiring all sorts of bad habits. In this internet age, one major problem is that of teenagers being glued to their mobile devices. If parents do not intervene in this obsession, they will deprive their children of vital things in life, such as exercise, conversation, adventure and reading. So with clothes, even though every teenager wishes to dress like their peers, there are occasions when it would be inappropriate for young girls, for example, to underdress or for young boys to be wrapped in shabby hoodies all the time. Parents should at least try to get their teenage children to learn about elegance and suitability. I sent mine off to the Victoria and Albert Museum to learn about the evolution of clothes and designs, and showed them movies starring Fred Astaire and Cary Grant in fabulously well-made suits, and Sophia Loren and Gina Lollobrigida in beautiful blouses and flaring skirts, worn with the slenderest of waists.

Children should also be told that, far from being an old fogey belief, mode of dress has been a tribal custom since humans found it necessary to wear clothes to suit the climate. That is why all tribes, both ancient and modern, take care to dress up, especially on ceremonial occasions. And they do so out of respect for tradition, which is the essential thread of history. Even Jeremy Corbyn, the UK's left-wing Labour leader, donned a white tie and tails, albeit reluctantly, at a state banquet. Of course, Corbyn is not a teenager, but on this occasion he seemed to have caved in to the metaphorical stare of Her Majesty as his mum.

My mother is in her late middle age but surprisingly appears to be much younger. My trouble and embarrassment is her dress sense – she will insist on wearing ripped jeans and chavvy leather jackets, especially when we go out to restaurants. How can I ask her to dress more appropriately for her age?

Leave her alone! We don't expect Ronnie Wood or Keith Richards to get into pathetic Dunhill suits. So why should you not let your mother behave like Suzi Quatro? I remember seeing her in concert in Canberra a few years ago when she was nearly 60 – all wrinkled, but looking great in leather and ripped jeans. It will be a sad day when you have to worry about your mother dressed like Golda Meir! Above all, never feel embarrassed about your mother. I will never forget crying as a boy watching *Imitation of Life*, in which Susan Kohner denied her mother because she was black and only a cook. You don't want that.

May I ask your advice about the suitability of tight jeans on men over 36 years of age? I am reaching my mid-70s and still have an enviable figure for a man of my age and have a suitcase full of trendy, admittedly fashionable and slim-cut tight black jeans which I am prone to wear. I find that my wardrobe is often commented on favourably by the opposite sex, but one friend (female) recently announced, in front of a house full of guests: 'Oh for goodness' sake – your jeans are FAR TOO tight.' I was embarrassed and so were the others around. Is it wrong to still be showing off one's figure at my age?

Yes.

• • •

I'm not an avid reader of your column. In fact, personally I find that your answers to readers are sometimes obnoxious. It seems you rarely have anything positive to contribute. Why is it that the human being is generally negative or oblivious to positives?

Because there are miserable people like you around, being generally negative; and being particularly negative when you are criticizing those who are negative.

TRAVELLING IN STYLE

'What, I wonder, is the protocol for bona fide
nudity on commercial flights?'

T**HE MODERN JET** – starting with the Boeing 707 and Douglas DC-8, and followed by the Boeing 747 – heralded the true beginning of our travels in the sky. Looking back at some of the old Pan American advertisements promoting its round-the-world trips, I was amused to notice that every passenger, old or young, was properly dressed: men in suits and ties, and women in blouses or dresses. Even the children were in their Sunday best. The stewardesses were even more pristine: each, like a cloud goddess, in starched uniform and with a meticulous coiffure. It was the heyday of the glamorous Pan Am girls, who served all those who travelled in style. In flight – without turbulence, it was claimed – passengers would enjoy fine dining, with gourmet foods and wines served on a trolley. Couples were even seen playing a game of chess, to demonstrate the stability of the flight. And so a gigantic industry of travelling in style was born.

Nowadays, however, with the Boeing 777 and 787 and Airbus's elephantine A380, air travel has dramatically changed from a luxury to a simple means of conveyance. The world is now open to everyone through affordable ticket prices. Hoi polloi became the target of budget airlines such as Laker, easyJet and Ryanair, and the hoodie seems to have become the most common form of air attire. On long-haul flights, I have hardly ever seen men wearing ties, or women in dresses. The idea of a special journey as peddled by Pan Am has long since evaporated. A plane journey is now as perfunctory as a bus ride, and aviation glamour has mostly been consigned to oblivion. That is, unless one is travelling first class or is in possession of a private jet.

First-class seats are now mostly in private partitioned spaces, and turn into fully flat beds with fluffy duvets. On Singapore Airlines, the two central seats convert into a double bed, presumably not designed for strangers. On Emirates Airlines, the space is installed with a mini-bar and a small dressing mirror, although the mini-bar is not refrigerated (an indictment on soft drinks), and one feels a little awkward with the vanity bulbs on either side of the mirror, unless one is Kenneth Branagh.

But ultimately, the most stylish travel comes with the private jet. There are, however, misconceptions about stylishness. For me, the most elegant aspect of travelling in a private jet is not boarding in haute couture with Goyard luggage, or even the total privacy, as craved by modern celebrities pursued by paparazzi. Rather, it is the painless check-in and check-out, contrasted with the trauma this normally brings to mind, and most of all the total flexibility of schedule (subject to that magic word 'slots') – plus, of course, the bonuses of smoking and of travelling with dogs, both of which are unthinkable on commercial flights. That said, all of these luxuries are best kept low-profile if one wants to remain 'stylish' oneself. There is nothing more vulgar than an owner bragging about taking their poodles on board, or being able to smoke a cigar in the cabin, or how the interior is decorated with leather and gold taps and how they could just hop on their craft at any time to go anywhere. The real stylishness of private travel is to keep quiet about these privileges and luxuries. And never to be condescending to those who travel private for the first time. Basic good manners and being considerate are the *sine qua non* of having style. So it is a misconception that money purchases style. On the contrary, money often destroys style.

Examples of such destruction are nowhere more evident than the plethora of super-yachts that has been built in the past two or three decades. Not only have these gin-palaces become ever flashier and uglier, echoing those massive cruise ships that look like dumpy blocks of faceless flats, but the interiors of most of these yachts, fetching tens or even hundreds of millions of dollars, have become homogeneous, uninspired and ultimately vapid. Such a pity that even brilliant marine architects are now taking orders from insipid owners and end up sacrificing elegance and beauty for extravagance and ostentation. The problem is that charm has been systematically consigned to oblivion: charm that exudes a sense of understated luxury and comfort and a frisson of magic; charm that is all quiet, unlike ostentatiousness, which is loud.

Look at luxury hotels nowadays. The lobby is invariably designed for the ostensible purpose of creating an impression, with lofty columns of marble and sweeping staircases. So they all look exactly like a hotel, which is a transient place, whereas the whole point of the entrance to a hotel is to invoke a sense of welcome, to make the guests feel as if they have come home – or at least to a place that feels like home. Immense lobbies of stone, therefore, with long, deep reception counters, are thoughtless designs. The Four Seasons Hotel in Hong Kong, for example, with its vast emptiness and huge columns, does not impress me one iota, whereas the Four Seasons Hotel in Milan, with its intimate atmosphere and stylish desks and chairs, appeals to me every time I am there. Yet a lot of people do not seem to appreciate the importance of intimacy and warmth, and regard a huge space with more marble than the Taj Mahal as being the apex of luxury. And why is marble found on the floor of every bathroom in every hotel? Marble must be the stupidest surface to have in a bathroom, because it becomes lethally slippery when wet. But designers and hoteliers consider it de rigueur, even though the towelling mats they provide are invariably too small and hardly ever cover the whole surface of the floor. How I wish that these lazy designers would spend more time studying the experiences of an end-user by staying in hotels themselves, before they impose their carelessness on us.

AIRPORTS

Going through security at the airport is now a standard procedure none of us can escape from, yet we often encounter rather obnoxious staff going through our stuff and often our bodies. How do we deal with the rude ones?

Airport security now constitutes the most unpleasant routine in our daily life. Richard Reid has a lot to answer for. He was the British 'shoe bomber' foiled trying to smuggle explosives in his sole on board a flight. As a result of his arrest in 2001, all of us who travel by air have had to suffer the indignity of taking our shoes off going through the detector. Imagine the numbers. Last year, about 3bn passengers went flying. So over the past 11 years, I estimate about 30bn have been affected. That means 60bn feet. Or 600bn toes! At an average of one inch per toe and two inches for the big ones, that would be 720bn inches of the human body which Reid has unwittingly affected. Arguably, he has been the world's most influential man in modern times.

Coupled with this unfortunate statistic are the 'security' staff, with their didactic attitude and keenness to exercise their petty authority, dispensing those prison-like plastic trays and taking out every item from passengers' bags with white gloves in slow motion, and molesting our contours with salacious familiarity – the female guards at Beijing airport are particularly vigilant and take 'touchy-feely' to new heights. Little wonder this modern torture has made the experience of air travel so irritating. Yet there is not much we can do. It is, in the short and long run, much more practical to surrender to the exercise of their little powers. It is annoying to see notices warning travellers that it is an offence to be abusive to any officer, when it makes no mention of their abuse to us.

Under the circumstances, my advice, sadly, is to be pragmatic and suffer all these small-minded gatekeepers and contrive as big a smile as one can in going through 'security'. Whatever one really thinks of them should be confined and contained either in the lining of one's stomach or in the incandescent veins of a clenched fist, best camouflaged – all to be bottled up in total monastic silence, until perhaps in the arrivals hall, when one might, as I often do, let out a primeval scream of shameful submission and utter despair.

How do you deal with some rather aggressive so-called 'security' people at the airport when they insist you take off your belt or shoes on a filthy floor, which seems rather undignified?

I always carry with me a 'blown-up' picture of a serious case of verrucas, which I then produce for the 'officer-in-charge', suggesting that if I took my shoes off and walked on the filthy floor, I might well catch this disease, for which I would hold them responsible. This at least causes them to be slightly flustered. And if they insist on taking one's belt off, one could pull a stunt by taking off one's trousers altogether. Mind you, one must have good legs and a snazzy pair of socks; or in the case of a woman, preferably fishnet stockings and suspenders.

You talked about airport security checks recently. I always set off the beeping alarm because I have bits of metal inside my body. Must I resign myself to the fact that I will always be searched?

I am afraid you will always be searched. Security 'guards' are not concerned with any legitimate alien parts inside your body. They just robotically follow the sounds of the beeps and aim to find things attached to the outside of your body. The army of female guards at Beijing airport is particularly vigilant. They thoroughly frisk both male and female passengers. Because I am very ticklish, I get the giggles when told to extend my arms horizontally, and they sweep their fingers firmly up my armpits, as they also do around my midriff. I must confess occasionally I feel a sense of frisson during these brief but intimate interludes with a stranger in uniform. When my wife is around, she is suspicious, seeing my raised eyebrows, squinted eyes and Popeye mouth.

Is it ever sensible to be sarcastic or funny in answering didactic questions from immigration or customs officers?

Not worth it. I once arrived in Sydney and was asked, 'Where are you coming from?', to which I replied, 'With warmth and love,' whereupon I was put in a room for an hour for being obstructive to an officer. But if you were to be terribly clever and witty, occasionally you might get away with it. The great Quentin Crisp, a declared homosexual at the time when it was a bit of a big deal, was once asked by a US immigration officer if he was a 'practising homosexual'. 'Certainly not,' Crisp replied, 'I am perfect at it.'

AEROPLANES

What are your thoughts about modern travel by commercial airlines and passenger liners?

I think the overall design of commercial aircraft, especially for those that openly declare themselves to be 'without frills', ought to be outlawed for the way they cram as many passengers as possible into the smallest possible space. They must think they are running a battery farm for chickens. It is all because of greed dressed up as utilitarianism – to achieve the greatest income from the greatest number of people paying the greatest amount of money. The argument for making travel accessible to the masses need not imply callousness. It is bad enough before boarding to have to go through 'security' like cattle in socks. The whole business of travel is now reduced to moving simply from A to B, without any sense of adventure or excitement.

In business and first class, for which the airlines charge like the Light Brigade, they should also offer more value for money. The loos, for example, have remained for years perfunctory and tight and plastic. Why can't so-called designers understand that it is more important to make the lavatory more luxurious than the cabin? And isn't it irritating when over-friendly crew come up and shake your hand, looking oleaginous, and committing to moronic propositions such as 'If there is anything at all you need, please let us know'? We have regressed considerably from the heydays of Pan Am 001, which remarkably was launched in the summer of 1947, whose luxury we can only glance at nowadays in the latest television series. People used to dress up properly to go on flights. Now you get appalling tracksuits and multicolour trainers, with unshaven men or haggard-looking women filing up and down the aisle like zombies, invariably mobilized by BlackBerrys and iPhones. Sometimes I feel like a cameo in *One Flew Over the Cuckoo's Nest*.

As for passenger liners, just think of the supreme elegance of the *Titanic* or the old *Queen Mary* or *Queen Elizabeth*, with majestic funnels that anchor a beautifully streamlined design. Yet nowadays shipbuilders and designers have continued to churn out grotesque-looking cruise monsters whose profiles resemble truncated parallelograms. The interiors of these so-called luxurious liners are enough to make me sick over three oceans. When I left Hong Kong at the tender age of 13, I remember boarding a small 20,000-tonne Greek liner that was by no means as luxurious as any run by the great P&O. But it had a sense of understated stylishness. We called at Colombo, Aden, Port Said and eventually Athens. It took 30 days. But I think if I had to endure that time in a modern monstrosity, I'd throw myself overboard after breakfast.

Is air travel getting better for passengers who want to go places more easily because of low costs? Or is there a price to pay for this opening of global destinations?

Economy travel has not improved with the mean amount of space airlines allow passengers to occupy. Their business model is to cram as many bodies as possible into a minimum space so as to generate the maximum amount of revenue.

It is worse with budget airlines, which arrogantly assume that passengers should have no right to demand any services to speak of.

On one budget flight, my father-in-law, who had Parkinson's disease, was treated appallingly and barked at to go to the back of the plane because he was not 'fit' to sit on the front row, which I had run and jostled hard to bag for him. How I wished to have been an 'air marshal' on that particular flight and had a gun to threaten those callous stewardesses with abundant make-up and stewards with nimble pointing fingers.

Window or aisle seat?

In economy class, always take the aisle seat, because it offers more room for one of your legs, if not both of them, whenever the trolley is not in service. This extra space, which should allow a lateral swing of about 25 degrees, could be precious if one already has luggage under the seat in front, thereby preventing one from stretching out one's legs. That is why those at the window or, worse still, in between the aisle seats in the middle are always worse off as regards manoeuvrability. In business or first class, the answer is more ambivalent, because both have much more comfortable seats, offering plenty of leg room, and the public aisle space need not be infringed upon. It also depends if one is travelling alone or with a companion. If solo, I would always want a window seat which maximizes privacy. A couple, however, might prefer the usual double configuration in the middle. Indeed, on Singapore Airlines, the two central seats can be converted into a double bed, which might particularly suit honeymoon couples, or those travelling with their dogs who claim they need 'emotional support', which is possible in certain jurisdictions, such as the US under its Air Carrier Access Act.

Your question also reminds me of my grandmother. In the 1970s, at the advent of long commercial flights, she wanted to visit us in England but was too scared to fly. So she took the *Canberra*, a grand P&O passenger liner that sailed all the way from Hong Kong to Tilbury. There were rough seas during the 30-day journey and my grandmother really hated the food and was utterly bored since she did not speak any English. So it was a very uncomfortable journey for her, and one that she did not want to repeat. So I told her that for her return trip to Hong Kong, I would fly with her and hold her hand and steady her nerves. I assured her that there was no danger in flying. After much persuasion, she agreed, but on the parting day she was far from calm. Without thinking, I gave her a window seat with myself on the aisle. I held her hand, which was cold, and repeated to her that she had no need to be afraid. 'But I am afraid,' she said. 'We are so high in the sky, just look at all those people below: they look like cockroaches!' I leaned over her and looked out the window. 'Grandma,' I said, 'they are cockroaches! We haven't taken off yet.'

If you want a large loo on a plane, you should try to fly on an Airbus A380, especially with one of the three big Middle

Eastern carriers. The bathrooms on those flying whales are huge and even come with showers in some cases. If given the option, would you ever try to shower at 38,000ft?

I have been on many A380s. On most of them, the loos are no larger than the standard ones you find in the old 747s or the newer 777s, or the smaller Airbuses. But it is true that on some Qatar and Emirates aircraft, the loos are twice as big and some of them have a shower inside. But I have no reason to go to the Middle East. I don't want to stop over in Dubai, however nefariously attractive it might be, nor Doha, nor Abu Dhabi, nor Bahrain. I would hesitate to use the showers because what happens if turbulence sets in when one has just soaped up? I wouldn't want to roll around in bubbled nakedness in mid-air at 38,000ft.

Also, the designers make the predictable mistake of using white light in the shower/loo, with the result that the whole facility feels like a utility and not a luxury. Talking of lighting, I hate the blue ultraviolet 'ambient' lighting that is used by a number of airlines. It feels like I am sleeping in a sunbed, faking a tan. Such purplish-blue light is best consigned to an Ibiza nightclub, choked with senseless dancers getting blind drunk or drugged up for their escapades from reality.

My girlfriend and I want to get married at Disney World in Orlando but her mother is afraid of flying. What would you do in this situation?

Practising as Sherlock Holmes, I would imagine you are a fairly sophisticated man of maturity offering to marry a rather uneducated but relatively beautiful and younger number than yourself. You seem to love her enough not to want to ridicule her screaming suburban disposition to marry at the utterly appalling Disney World in Florida. You also appear to want to please her by trying to arrange for her mother to attend the wedding, despite the Atlantic Ocean and her aviophobia.

The answer is surely to put them both in the best stateroom on the *QE2*, or one of those equally vast liners of parochial ostentation, and sail across the Atlantic in style. Then you can collect them in a luxurious Winnebago in Noo Yawk and motor them down all the way to Florida, calling on Charleston and Savannah, whose charm might just awaken any seedlings of taste in mother and daughter.

So spoil them both to death. It's your mid-life crisis! Is there any other way to demonstrate lust for your young bride?

Do you wear the sleeper suits provided on commercial flights or do you keep them packaged in case they come in useful as presents?

I don't ever get into the airline sleeper suits because they are not large enough for my frame. In particular, I hate the elastic waistbands, which are constrictive for those of us who harbour a proper midriff beneath our trousers. It is also tiresome to have to change into them in the tiny loos which are standard on airlines, making the process resemble an escape routine by Houdini. So I get on flights with my own loose trousers with drawstrings that I can easily calibrate and soft shirts to assimilate a decent pair of pyjamas in Egyptian cotton.

But when I founded Shanghai Tang I did supply Cathay Pacific with our beautiful pyjamas for its first-class cabins. They were very popular because they were silk and designed to be comfortably loose, and passengers would keep them afterwards. In those days it was lovely to see a flying dormitory replete with one's own designed clothes.

As for the wash kits given out in first and business class, I never keep them because they don't offer Euthymol toothpaste.

But these complimentary pouches were very attractive to the late Duke of Marlborough, known as 'Sunny', who famously hoarded them to be recycled as Christmas presents.

You are absolutely right about the quality of the food offered today on trains and most airlines. That is the reason why many people now carry their own snacks on the go. Mr Twit, for instance, has been doing this for a while. According to Roald Dahl, he always keeps some cornflakes and little lumps of sardine and cheese inside his beard. How clever!

Sorry, but Mr Twit was a horrible person who did not 'keep' some cornflakes and lumps of sardines and cheese in his dirty beard. These were leftovers slovenly stuck to his beard. So I do not think that any one of us who wishes to be prudent against bad food being served on public transport would do so by trying to imitate Mr Twit.

If I have time, I always try to take on board with me a couple of decent sandwiches, preferably made with Mother's Pride white bread, which is artificially chewy and absolutely delicious. The secret is to cut each slice into four small squares so that they can be taken discreetly in single mouthfuls.

Having recently endured a 12-hour flight sitting next to two alternately crying babies who artfully prevented me from finding sleep, I wondered how would a gentleman such as yourself have reacted, confronted by such parenting incompetence?

Being a gentleman implies being extra considerate and polite. And therefore I would simply put in my earplugs and keep quiet. After all, the commercial flight is public transport, and anyone who pays is entitled to exercise normal human behaviour which, in the case of a baby, is to cry. I was once woken on the plane by a fellow passenger who accused me of snoring too loudly in the cabin. I assure you that I read him my rights and challenged him to a duel on arrival, as I try to be a gentleman to the last.

I have been flying for longer than I care to remember and as soon as the plane takes off I press the recline button and settle into a more comfortable angle. However, more than one impertinent passenger has had the temerity to point out that I should not recline the seat until after the seatbelt sign has been switched off. I've always told myself that they are wrong and the sign is to let people know they can start walking about the plane. So I thought this was a question that must be put to the oracle, though such incidents may not concern those who fly first class!

Of course I fly economy (Dear Reader, in the interest of accuracy I would like to point out that this absurd claim is based on there being but one class on Tang's borrowed private jet – Ed.) and know exactly your inclination. Allow me to let you in on a procedure I have found mostly successful. The secret is to perform the reclining with a series of imperceptible moves. For preparation, you must tense up your entire torso so that when you depress the reclining button, you only edge backwards to the tiniest degree before releasing the button. Repeat these small movements up to a dozen times, performing them with total stealth. It is vital to start this creep as soon as the plane accelerates on take-off, so that when the aircraft starts to incline the passenger behind will least, or not at all, notice the back of your seat reclining. By the time the plane reaches cruising altitude, your position will be a fait accompli.

I once boarded a plane only to find another passenger already sat in my assigned seat, looking settled with a drink in hand and reading a newspaper. I was rather annoyed and demanded my seat back. Should I have been more polite?

You must always try to be as polite as possible. Exactly the same thing happened to me once and I simply joked that maybe I should have taken her seat instead. On asking to see her boarding pass, I discovered she should have been in 41A, not 1A. I found out later that when she had shown her boarding pass at the door, her thumb had covered up the figure '4'. On a contrasting occasion, I once sprinted across the runway with a 'Speedy Boarding' pass for easyJet and scrounged the aisle seat on the front row, only to be told later that it was reserved for one of the crew and that I had to go right to the back of the plane. I was not polite then.

On a commercial flight, is one obliged to be polite and talk to one's neighbours? Or is it better to keep oneself to oneself?

I avoid talking to anyone adjacent to me on a flight, especially on long-haul flights. Indeed I go out of my way not even to catch the eye of my fellow passengers lest they become tediously loquacious. I once sat next to the delectable actor Julia Roberts on Concorde, however. I tried for hours across the Atlantic to catch her eye in order to strike up a conversation, but without the remotest success, and ended up too pathetic to have uttered a single syllable to her. She must have stuck fast to my own principle of maximum avoidance of strangers.

An idea for naturists: on those dreadful 14-hour flights, why not disrobe and wander the aisles?

I would love to see that, although in all my years of air travel covering millions of miles, I have never witnessed such behaviour. I suspect it is likely to be illegal as it is bound to cause disruption among passengers. But what if the nudity were executed with total calmness and pacifism, with no sign of provocation? I would laugh out loud if I were confronted by naked bodies sauntering down the aisle, although if I was just opening my eyes from a slumber, the immediate sensation might be rather disconcerting, particularly in that dreamy, ambient blue light. And what happens if naturists were to travel together en masse for, say, one of their annual conventions? It would be hilarious to see a group of them starkers, sitting or moving around in the cabin. Would the stewards and stewardesses continue to serve them peanuts and drinks? What, I wonder, is the protocol for bona fide nudity on commercial flights?

HOTELS

What things do you insist on having in a hotel room?

This is a stupid question because it clearly requires further context before it is properly answerable. A room at an airport hotel for a few hours of rest between connecting flights? Or a room merely used to sleep in while business meetings are done all day outside? Or a room on holiday for a stay of a week or two? Without these contexts, it is meaningless to answer the question. The reason so many hotel rooms are badly designed is because they are done precisely without proper reference to context.

If there were one thing I'd like most in any hotel room, in any context, it would be romance. Take the small top suite, at the dilapidated Grand Hotel in Tangier, in which Matisse painted many of his Moroccan paintings looking across to Europe from the shores of Africa. Or the Churchill Suite at La Mamounia in

Marrakech from where you can smell an olive grove but see a snow-capped Atlas mountain across the desert. Yes, a room with a view. Forster got it in one.

Is it just me or do other hotel guests request that cushions not be put on the bed? Most hotels have done away with bedspreads, thank God, but they persist with these impertinent decorative items that carry more in the way of germs than aesthetic value. I imagine guests using them for whatever need pops up and, otherwise, tossing them on the floor. The first thing I do is remove them and write a note to the hotel maid asking her to keep them off the bed.

I couldn't agree with you more. I detest large cushions on the bed. They are instantly flung to the ground by me. What I can't understand is how a professional interior designer paid by an established hotel could think that such cushions add decorative atmosphere to the room? Another highly irritating discovery is when the duvet is tightly tucked into the end of the mattress, which is the usual practice in all hotels. Doesn't anyone in housekeeping know that a duvet should be treated differently from blankets, which do need to be tucked in? Trying to yank the duvet up from under the mattress to cover one's head is a screaming constant for me.

Thank you for confirming that I am not the only person in the world driven bananas by hotel duvets being tucked in. I have simply no idea what would possess somebody to do something that is not only irritating but pointless.

The problem about a duvet tucked in like a blanket in a made-up bed is that it is almost impossible to untuck it once you get into the bed, unless you have calf muscles like Linford Christie. And because it is tucked in, it becomes too short to cover one's face, which, for some of us who like to sleep with our head inside a duvet, is highly irritating.

I once stayed in Van Diemen's Land (Tasmania), which did not record the finest moments in Australian history regarding the Aborigines. Add to this the frightening legends of the last Tasmanian tigers. As a result, I was absolutely petrified in the darkness of my bedroom and only wanted to crouch under my duvet all night. So housekeeping in hotels should sacrifice neatness and let the edges of a duvet flow freely over the bed.

Regarding your recent comments about hotel cushions, I thought you would be amused/appalled by what awaited me after checking in yesterday at an otherwise exceptional Oslo hotel: I counted nine specimens on a queen-sized bed . . . and a spare in the cupboard.

I would, as the hotel is in Oslo, check in with that Nordic monster the Kraken and let it loose on the wretched cushions. As the creature resembles a giant squid, it should have eight arms and two tentacles, enough to deal with all 10 cushions. If you were to discover more than 10 cushions, I would suggest you locate from Greece a Lernaean Hydra, which has multiplying heads. This monster should be able to hoover up any number of cushions and dump them in the Underworld.

Why do we get chocolates on pillows in hotels? It's even sillier than the whole turn-down rigmarole or the cushion extravaganza that you've rightly pilloried recently. They wish us 'sweet dreams', or words to that effect. Why not just say 'Enjoy this complimentary gumrot as you sleep'?

I have always subscribed to the theory that if Austrians, especially Austrian women, did not eat as much chocolate before going to bed, Freud would not have been able to lure them to his chaise longue for Oedipus-this and Oedipus-that, and become so famous. The fact is that chocolate seems to intensify the occurrence of dreams. So don't underestimate that small piece of dark matter, or 'gumrot', as you call it, on the pillow, for it was the acorn of an entire branch of psychoanalysis.

But on a practical level, leaving food on the bed could attract all sorts of unsavoury insects, especially bedbugs. I was astonished to find recently that it is now a standard provision in all lease agreements in New York that the landlord must undertake that there are no insects in their furnished beds. Maybe you can start a campaign against chocolate, threatening to sue the hotel on the basis of a possible invasion of insects. That would bring the petit bourgeois practice to an immediate halt – although, alas, we are too late in reversing the fame of Dr Sigmund Freud.

I was wondering what your view would be of making a light packed lunch from the breakfast buffet of a hotel?

There are three good reasons why you should have no qualms about filtering food from a hotel breakfast buffet for your packed lunch:

(1) It was more or less what happened in that most beautiful film, *Elvira Madigan*, starring that most beautiful Swedish actress Pia Degermark. Therefore, if only on grounds of reflected aesthetics, your action might be regarded as beautiful. (Mind you, the protagonists of that film committed suicide afterwards.)

(2) My mother-in-law, I am told by my wife, does it all the time as she travels up and down the country on her regular excursions with her companion. I am always rather excited by the

prospect of her being caught one day, although this is not likely to happen, as she has apparently perfected her sleight of hand over the breakfast buffet to an art form.

(3) There is always so much waste from hotel buffets and it is a particularly unpleasant sight to see greedy guests piling food on their plates. Your packed lunch by stealth would reduce both obesity and waste. Also, it brings a frisson of excitement to breakfast when you act like a pilferer.

· · ·

I write just to say that I enjoy your column. Sometimes it is a little difficult to believe that some of the questions are real, but you cannot make them up, can you?

Remember what Jesus said to doubting St Thomas: 'Blessed are they that have not seen, and yet have believed.' I do not make up my own questions. They are all genuine. Indeed, there are too many of them for me to answer. But annoyingly, a lot of the questions are far too long; and to use the better ones, I often have to start pretending to behave like the French with the guillotine. I do urge correspondents to brandish Occam's razor!

RELATIONSHIPS

'What better choice for a romantic dinner à deux than a couple of Cornish pasties at a railway station?'

WHEN MY GREAT-GRANDFATHER emigrated to Hong Kong from Canton, he accumulated one wife and five concubines, partly to show off his prosperity, which has long been a traditional Chinese custom. He cleverly built a house seven storeys high and installed his wife and concubines in ascending order: the official wife living on the ground floor, concubine no. 1 on the first floor, concubine no. 2 on the second, and so on. Each week, he would start by spending Monday with his wife, and then steadily climb the floors throughout the remaining days of the week, staying with each of his string of concubines in turn. On Sundays he would be at the penthouse on the top floor, resting. Fortunately for my great-grandfather, polygamy – where concubines were regarded as wives – was allowed in Hong Kong at this time, and similar arrangements were widespread. Indeed, my grandfather also took on concubines, because polygamy was not made unlawful in Hong Kong until as late as 1971. My biological grandmother was also a concubine. So I am the product of two concubines, before my mother, thankfully, married my father, a monogamist. Otherwise, I might well have been a triple illegitimate child!

I had always wondered how a polygamous household got on, and remember asking both my great-grandmother and grandmother about their relationships with the wives and other concubines. Surprisingly, they both told me that they seemed to get on fairly well together, principally because Chinese women were willingly submissive to the husband. At least until he died. Then there would often be an almighty fight over his estate, when civility among the wives and concubines dispersed abruptly.

Maybe it is easier to sustain a monogamous marriage because, theoretically at least, the husband has to concentrate on only one wife, rather than a stable of concubines. However, judging by the ever-increasing number of divorces, it's clear that even a simple bilateral relationship is fraught with difficulties. The problem seems to be rooted in the belief that there is eternal romance in a marriage union, and that all the frisson of court-ship will last beyond the wedding day. If truth be told, the routine and habit of marriage can take its toll on the ambitious promise of 'till death us do part' long before the seven-year itch sets in. No wonder that the more we allow a marriage to drift into staleness, the more likely it will break down. Couples have to work on bringing 'freshness' to the marital home, because in order to sustain a long relationship, it is important to punctuate it with a little excitement, just like introducing a new line of products in a retail business. It's no coincidence that Zara, with its constantly changing range of products, is such a phe-nomenal success and that its customers keep coming back for more and more.

Accordingly, husbands and wives should devise new activities and avoid lazy patterns of behaviour. Instead of going out to your favourite restaurant, go instead to, say, a train station for supper. There is a particularly good pasty shop at King's Cross: buy two pasties in a brown paper bag, along with a couple of cans of Diet Coke, and sit on a bench and watch all the passen-gers and greeters come and go, in that vast amphitheatre of romances and break-ups, laughter and tears, partings and re-unions. I assure you that it's no less enjoyable a pastime than sipping coffee in a café on the pavement of a Parisian avenue, watching the world go by.

I would also like to mention another kind of relationship: the one between best friends. I have often heard how best friends must be able to rely on each other for succour at times of trouble, because the relationship is based on a great deal of accumulated give-and-take. But this way of thinking cannot be right. When we befriend someone and do favours for them, or give them presents, or go out of our way to please them, we should do so voluntarily and never expect anything in return. Best friends are better viewed as a one-way street, not a two-way street. I have often said to my children and others that we are what we give, not what we are given.

DATING

I am authoritatively informed that at a well-known upmarket supermarket in Halkin Street, London, one can pick up the best of fresh food and also, apparently, the pick of single attractive liquid men who are not dentally or follicly [*sic*] challenged. But for 10 months I have been surprisingly unsuccessful. Could it be that the contents of one's trolley actually matter? And, if so, can you direct me as to what comestibles might spark the fire that screams? Yes, I am alone and available for dinners, lunches and, perhaps later, breakfast.

Stop screaming, especially to yourself! Romance cannot be sought. Still less would you find it in a supermarket. I don't know why you should choose one in fancy Belgravia. Presumably you think that the men whom you meet there will be more eligible and attractive and wealthy. But eligible and attractive and wealthy men don't actually shop at supermarkets. If you were to find a smart-looking man taking an interest in you, he is more likely than not to be a cad or a bounder whose motive would be exactly the same as yours in trying to catch someone of the opposite sex who is eligible and attractive and wealthy.

It is a blessing in disguise that you have not had any success, because being approached there and taken out to dinner and smooched is likely to end in disaster – with or without your mascara and rouge. Certainly it won't be love.

You are better off with Tesco in Surbiton, the Mecca of suburbia.

On behalf of a 'friend', I am writing to ask you if, in your opinion, it is U or non-U to use online dating websites. I have been assured by several 'clever' and 'modern' friends of mine that EVERYONE is DOING IT.

The biggest problem I have with dating websites is the question of verisimilitude. Of course we ask for photographs, and when we get excited with the looks, we ponce ourselves up, like Lee Marvin in *Cat Ballou*, for our date, only to discover a rather large gap between the photograph and reality. Against such unbearable shocks, I would not touch these websites, whether or not they are U or non-U. And if everyone is doing it, I would, *a fortiori*, avoid it. But if you really have to use it, I suggest that you send out your worst photograph. That way, if you were to receive a response, you might yet find true love.

What should a woman do if a man gives her jewellery as a present that she does not like? Keeping silent might encourage more presents like that which would not be enjoyed and would be a waste, but pointing out the fact of dislike is also rude. I have never expressed my dislike, but my friend did and her boyfriend just bought her a different piece instead. What do you advise?

I advise first that you might consider trying to go out with your friend's boyfriend. He seems to be more in tune than your own!

If that proves difficult, you must not hesitate to tell your boy-friend that you don't like what he gives you, and might as well kill two birds with one stone by specifying what you do like. What's the point of a relationship if you can't maximize its brutal honesty? Besides, it's a waste of his money, which might well be yours one day! When my wife gives me things that I don't like, which is rare because she is a clever girl, I will tell her straight and straightaway so that she might think a bit straighter next time. This un-uxorial behaviour might be sneered at in the occidental feminist world, but it's not yet treated with contempt in the Orient. And believe it or not, my wife, who comes from Essex, actually enjoys bringing me my slippers.

Oh dear, oh dear – the vagaries of youth. What is the form when greeting an old lover (or even, dare I say, a one-night stand from the sands of time) in public at a party – fulsomely and unabashed? And without allowing the look on my face to show too cruelly the memory of too much Blue Nun and desperation?

I would adopt a blunter approach: go straight up to your ex and say something like: 'I know it has been a long time, and I know that you must have been agonizing over your mistake of leaving me. To show how magnanimous I am, I am willing to forgive your stupidity and give you another chance. You will have to take me away now, and we must start with an evening at the Ritz. And I want that diamond ring from Graff that you did not buy me all those years ago. Then I want houses in London and Hampshire, and an account at Hoare with £100,000 to start with. If you promise me all that now and show complete contrition, I will consider having you back.' As they say, 'You don't ask, you don't get!' Just remember Bridget Jones.

A very good friend recently 'by accident' told a girl (whom I have been seeing for the past two years, he also knows) that I already have a wife. I lost this girl after that. What should I do with this friend? Please advise.

If he really did not mean to spill the beans on you, then you should do nothing. Not only because he is your good friend, but because sooner or later your girlfriend will find out you are cheating on her as well as your own wife. Hiding one's wife in any affair is doomed to failure because a time bomb eventually blows up. You might even thank your friend for his inadvertence, for he must have effectively saved you a lot of money and lying, although not in bed.

ROMANTIC GESTURES

I need to woo a lovely girl, who has mentioned that she adores classical piano. What pieces are the most romantic, or indeed erotic? I am a beginner player but intend to practise and impress her with a recital.

On reincarnation, I would, without a heartbeat, want to be an outstanding concert pianist, because I know that it is the most extraordinary life one could have. But being a total amateur in real life, I would definitely caution you against learning a piece to impress your girl. As a total acolyte, you are bound to make a mess of a performance. Your extra anxiety will guarantee a cock-up.

Yet if you were to be really determined, I could suggest Satie's 'Gymnopédie No. 1', which is not impossible for a beginner to learn. And because it is quintessentially French, it just falls short of being syrupy. Maybe you could also try Schumann's 'Träumerei'. I heard the mighty Horowitz play it as an encore once, which of course surprised everyone since the piece is usually learned by a beginner. If you choose this piece, you could mention that Horowitz played it, which always sounds good.

Otherwise, I would suggest you get practising, and try holding on to your girl for, say, five years, after which you might just be competent enough to play Scriabin – for his music is as erotic as they come in the bedroom.

What would your view and advice be on men presenting lingerie as a gift to wives, lovers or girlfriends? Having been the recipient of such gifts in the latter categories, I have mixed feelings, having been charmed and revolted.

My advice for men is to stay clear of trying to buy lingerie for women. We cannot understand the points of comfort, say, given our different human contours. More to the point, why fuss over a garment which is, presumably, hoped to come off fairly fast? In reverse, when I first opened my shop Shanghai Tang I sold a couple of silk boxer underpants to the gloriously beautiful Cindy Crawford for her boyfriend. She seemed to know exactly what she wanted and never asked for any advice, contrary to what I would do if I entered a lingerie shop.

On sending flowers to a young lady – was it de trop to send a note along with them which I dictated to my personal assistant and which I topped and tailed? I am forced to muse that perhaps a handwritten note in its entirety might have had a more favourable outcome.

Never send flowers to someone you fancy with a note. It is a more stylish way to express one's affections since anonymity breeds intrigue – an important ingredient of romance. And when you don't get a fairly swift reply, you know you are in competition with other suitors.

What is the most stylish way in which to celebrate Valentine's Day? Are there any no-nos that must be avoided?

A table at a dark bistro, with a candlelit dinner on a chequered tablecloth in red and white, served by a French waiter speaking in accented English, has to be a no-no. For a thoroughbred romantic dinner, it must depend on cerebral activities and preferably a surprise, for romance is all in the mind and not to be conflated with sentimentality, which requires some material reminder.

I always find that a very romantic place for dinner à deux is at a railway station with its history of encounters and separations – that vast receptacle of human emotions across a spectrum of intensities, whispered or touched, lachrymose or in laughter. The food and drinks are really cameo to the occasion, because when we are in love, we are not sustained by bodily appetite.

Once on Valentine's Day at King's Cross, I got a couple of Cornish pasties and cans of Diet Coke and ate them together with my future wife on a bench, watching all the passers-by as if they were the players from Shakespeare's stage of the seven ages. We would try to identify the lover, 'sighing like furnace, with a woeful ballad made to his mistress' eyebrow'. And for moments of lesser erudition, we would play the game of 'lookalike' and pick out strangers who resembled people we knew, which never failed to generate laughter.

The film *Brief Encounter* is not a bundle of laughs but one that oozes sadness and that plague of unrequited love, yet it defines, with a little help from Rachmaninov's second piano concerto pounding in the background, the potency of a railway station as a backdrop to a romantic interlude.

Another good Valentine's Day venue in London would be anywhere that has a view of the Tower of London, for it was here that the Duke of Orléans, imprisoned after the Battle of Agincourt, wrote perhaps the first documented Valentine's message – to his wife. He began in a whining poem: 'I am already sick of love, My very gentle Valentine . . .' You can then impress your beloved with this moving tale, pointing to the Tower. If I were Jude Law, I would do this, as he is playing Henry V and could boast that it was he who was arguably responsible for initiating the Valentine practice from one of his prisoners.

Following my recommendation of a Cornish pasty and a can of Diet Coke on a bench at King's Cross station as a suitable St Valentine's dinner, I have received several alternative suggestions for venues, such as the restaurant at Spean Bridge station on the line to Fort William, Scotland, and the oyster bar at Grand Central in New York.

I have never been to the former, although I might have glimpsed it once when I went to Fort William to stay at Inverlochy Castle, a hotel that is supposedly the epitome of Scottish luxury, which, given the legendary tightness of the Scots, might sound like an oxymoron.

As for the oyster bar at Grand Central, which I have been to, I admit the station has one of the most splendid interiors of modern times. The only trouble is the obvious association of the oyster as an aphrodisiac, which might send a presumptuous message to the girl. And would she even enjoy slurping up a slimy lump that is still on the move and taking its last breath? How anticlimactic it would be if she were to pass on the oyster and opt for the much duller plate of smoked salmon or prawn cocktail? Much simpler to leave food out of it.

My main point is to appreciate utilitarian spaces such as King's Cross, with its draughty promise of yet draughtier destinations, without the slightest hint of anything fancy, thereby creating a real juxtaposition of ostensible dullness and cerebral excitement that never fails to intensify our sense of romance.

Is it acceptable to send Valentine's cards to one's pets?

For pet lovers, yes, as long as we make believe that our pets would appreciate them. I once wrote out a few cards for our three dogs and bird, posted them to our home, received them on their behalf and placed them near where they slept. The following morning I found one card inside our cockatoo's cage chewed up and spat out, and another used as a pit-stop mat for our Jack Russell puppy.

I remember trying to convince myself that these animal reactions must not be interpreted in human terms – imagine if overnight my wife chewed up and spat out my Valentine's card! I haven't really bothered to send another batch of cards to my pets, if only for fear of confronting ingratitude.

HAPPY MARRIAGE

What is the best advice for a man greeting his wife on his return from work? Is a kiss essential? What else might be considered as good manners or wise behaviour?

How many film scenes have we all seen of the husband letting himself in the front door with his jangling keys and putting his briefcase down in the hallway and shouting out the name of his wife and then kissing her lovingly? I suppose this syrupy image of domestic bliss has set the standard for spousal greetings after a hard day's work. But how excruciatingly middle class that would be. I always try to come home before my wife or while she is out so that she can demonstrate her affection for me when she comes home. The late-comer invariably feels guilty.

Mind you, it is always a bit tricky when a husband returns home much later than the wife expects. Does he explain? And just a little or fully confess? Might a kiss be construed as an act of contrition or a gesture of Judas? If one has anything to hide, one must keep an ambivalent smiling face. The Germans are very practical and have a specific word, *Drachenfutter*, for a gift presented to one's wife as an apology for being out late. The word literally means 'dragon fodder'. We men should learn from this cleverly pre-emptive action.

My wife favours living in a large house in the country, whereas I would prefer a small apartment in London. Predictably, we rattle around in a substantial property in the heart of Dorset, with all that this entails in terms of mud, social deprivation and inconvenience. Short of divorce or buying a second property, can you suggest a compromise that is less one-sided than our present arrangement?

Rent a house in London with a bit of garden, and encourage your wife to come up to stay, so that she doesn't think that living in London must consist of being boxed up in a small concrete flat. By feeling a bit of space, especially if you choose somewhere on the edge of London, such as, say, Richmond, she might be persuaded to abandon your pile in Dorset. Mind you, Virginia Woolf once said: 'If I had to choose between Richmond and death, I'd choose death.'

I was told by my ex-father-in-law that the key to a good marriage is to keep surprising your wife. This pearl of

wisdom came too late for his daughter and me, but works very well with my second wife! What would you suggest is a unique surprise that an uxorious man can give to his wife?

As surprises can be both pleasant and nasty, you must have given your ex-wife the latter kind, which would explain your first divorce. For your present wife, I would suggest that you follow the example of Sir Philip Green, who should be made the patron saint of uxoriousness, by handing over everything you have to your wife. Just ask your solicitor today to assign to her all of your cash and assets. That would certainly be a pleasant surprise to any wife. No wonder Lady Green always looks supremely happy! But if you want to topple Sir Philip and be uber-uxorious, you might add a multiple organ-donor declaration and volunteer to give away your eye, heart, liver and kidney, all of which to be distributed according to the wishes of your wife, for her family, friends, strangers or even lovers.

My petite and pretty Peruvian wife of 45 years (married) is a notoriously slow eater – much to the chagrin of hovering waiters bent on early plate removal and dinner guests craving dessert. While my dear wife picks at her plate, savouring every morsel, I being Irish am a gobbler. We would like your advice.

Simple: order only a main course for your wife, and for yourself three or four courses and arrange to start together. If your wife protests and insists on a full three-course repast, then you have two choices: either you yourself should go for six or seven courses, or you bring something like a book and pace yourself between reading and munching. When my wife brings a book she can't put down at mealtime, I produce my *Times* crossword, which I try every day. If none of these works, then arrange with the restaurant to serve your wife each of the courses in, say, three equal portions. She will soon become bored by the same lots and should become a faster eater. You would then be training her like a mouse with a piece of cheese in scientific experiments.

Where do you stand on TVs in the master bedroom? This was a topic of heated debate at a recent dinner party. One camp was purist – a bedroom is for sleeping and lovemaking. The other perspective was the national news should be conveniently the last thing to do each night. My wife and I manage both. Is this dangerous, mixing the two?

You must let on to all our readers your secret formula of making love while watching the news! My wife watches the news in order to avoid me. For my part, as we prepare for bed, I tend to suggest a bit of comedy, as I wish to laugh before I sleep – and she doesn't disagree with that. Thankfully, just looking at each other often does the trick. Going back to my youth, I can testify to the usefulness of a television set in the bedroom for nascent courting: put on a horror movie, and a girl will volunteer to snuggle up to you, burying her face into your boomerang arm and sensitive shoulder. So I am all for a television set in a bedroom, although I have been told by many reliable sources that its main reason is for pornography. The proof of this is that any hotel room nowadays offers an adult channel for which one has to pay. But we tend to forget that we don't have to switch the television on. And when a television set is switched off, it's not there.

As a married Asian woman with a primarily Western upbringing, I would like to seek your advice on how best to

respond to a very hands-on and nosy mother-in-law who calls several times a week and needs to know every detail of our weekly schedule.

If you love your husband who loves his mother and loves you to love his mother, then you must suffer your mother-in-law and be nice to her and do as she tells you. This is the submissive attitude of the Chinese tradition at least. But if you love your husband who loves you more than his own mother, then you and your husband could join forces to repel the domestic invasion of your mother-in-law, because you would then be lending full support to your husband, which is also the Chinese way. If you don't, however, love your husband, this is the chance for you to be belligerent to your mother-in-law and find ways to deceive and unnerve her so that she becomes upset and complains to your husband, who will then complain to you, thereby intensifying your loveless marriage. This also falls in with the Chinese tradition of being cunningly Machiavellian in achieving what you want, viz. a divorce.

FRIENDS

What is the best way of dealing with a friend who is a pathological social and corporate climber? Do you know anyone afflicted similarly – and can I tell them that that is what they are? What is the form?

Send them a copy of Ovid's *Metamorphoses*, in which the plight of the over-ambitious Icarus is told. If your egotists don't get it, send them images of Bruegel's *Landscape with the Fall of Icarus*. Maybe also the magnificent *The Lament for Icarus* by Draper. Or give them, as their birthday or Christmas present, a powder compact with 'Icarus' in rouge scrawled across its mirror. If, after all this, your friends are still puzzled, they will be, in my estimation, beyond redemption.

When a friend comes to stay the weekend and all she talks about is herself, she is quite entertaining, but by Sunday you feel that she hasn't bothered to ask anyone else how they are, or even taken note that her reason for visiting was to see a newborn baby – whom she hasn't even noticed. Can you advise?

The most disarming effect you can have on people who talk about themselves all the time is to turn away and ignore them, preferably mid-sentence. You should conspire to do this with your family and friends. Very soon, the loquacious culprit should notice that verbosity is never a magnet, but a repellent. On this particular occasion, you could go even further by leaving the baby in her arms and pinching the little one to make sure that it cries, so that your friend is distracted from talking about herself.

My wife and I asked an old friend to be godfather to our eldest child and he agreed. Since then, however, he's quit his job and has not worked for two years. To boot, he has generally become unreliable in all respects. We regret our decision and would like to choose someone else now. What should we do?

You should immediately relate the biblical story of the prodigal son to your child so that your child will live in hope that the godfather will come right again. This will conveniently instil a sense of charity and tolerance on the part of the child, making you not only a good father but a good surrogate godfather. I am afraid that as a godfather to 31 godchildren myself, I have not been exactly meticulous in discharging all of my individual duties, and so I hesitate to plead mitigation towards derelictions by godparents. Indeed, I can tell you that a few parents have made it known to me that they had appointed 'honorary' god-parents in my place and distaste. (What a beautiful zeugma!) Therefore, you might do the same. Get someone richer and more dependable and substitute your wayward friend by an 'honorary' godparental appointment, in case the prodigal son does not limp back.

A good friend (since university days) recently married someone I find simply ghastly. Despite many attempts to warm to her out of loyalty to my mate, it's apparent she is indeed completely unbearable to more people than just myself. It seems sad to let our friendship drift but I see no other options. I've tried to keep to 'boys' lunches' and the like but invariably he wants to involve her. Any suggestions greatly appreciated.

I have several friends who are married to ghastly spouses. It's easier when your friends are male because at least you can then contrive to have business lunches and meetings and games of poker with them, and avoid their wives. But it is trickier if your friends are female, because then the ghastly husbands might think you are trying to have an affair with their wives – which might even be the case.

Then the cunning thing to do is to pretend by ingratiating yourself to the husband, so that he grows to like you and trust you and won't mind that you see his wife. This approach is based on the inscrutable tactic that 'If you can't beat them, then beat them just as they think you are going to join them'!

I have a very good friend who has bought a large house in the country and spent a great deal of money and time decorating it. He has asked me to be one of his first guests, and I am not entirely sure that I will like any of his decorations because I don't like his taste. Should I be honest and tell him my true feelings, which might hurt his, or should I skirt around my opinions and be polite?

Of course the principle is that you should be utterly true to your friends. Indeed, it often takes a really good friend to tell an ugly truth. But in matters of taste, 'truth' is possibly manoeuvrable. If I were you, I would sing his praises for things you like, but be reticent on things you don't. If you were pressed on things you don't like, you might choose to use an understatement or even a litotes with which to express your sentiment – something like: 'I am not entirely sure that I wouldn't have hung that painting elsewhere . . .' or 'If I were forced to choose an alternative colour, I might not have stayed with grey.' On your first visit, you ought to adopt this polite approach. After all, there is no reason why you shouldn't be polite to your friends. If he is clever, he will pick up your nuances and appreciate your politeness. If he is stupid and does not detect any of your ironic remarks, then even better that he should assume your approval. Over time, you can smuggle your criticisms in a gradual crescendo. But of course there is the school of thought that one ought to be totally brutal with one's good friends. So if you really don't like what you see, you might just bluntly say to him: 'This is all ghastly – how could you have possibly wasted all that time and money?' But this frontal attack requires a very strong armour of friendship to withstand.

An acquaintance has self-published a book of such turgid illiteracy and such outstanding tripe that it is best used for

firewood – how does one skirt the issue by not actually admitting that it is for the bin?

If you don't want to be offensive or you wish to be polite, simply write back and say thank you, adding the words: 'I much look forward to reading it.' Then you must keep silent. If pressed further, or if ambushed by an accidental meeting, then say something like: 'Oh, I have it next to my bed, and I would have finished it but for the recent diagnosis of my sleep apnoea.'

I wonder if you can advise me about a friend who, whenever he sees a piano – no matter where he is – sits down and plays his set piece with his foot firmly held down on the loud pedal. He has one piece in his repertoire (Rachmaninov, about six bars in total) and it is frankly excruciating. How can I tell him?

Lock your piano next time he comes. And if he protests, tell him that he cannot go round with a pathetic repertoire of six bars of anything. Or invite somebody who is in fact very good to perform before your friend so that he might feel, in comparison, that he has acute arthritis. Talking of showing off, everyone interested in the piano must watch the phantasmagorical competition between two pianists in the 1998 film *The Legend of 1900* in which the winner hit the notes so hard that he was able to light a cigarette off the strings, which were practically on fire. Tell your friend that unless he plays like that, he shouldn't bother. By the way, you must not show your own ignorance by calling the sustaining pedal 'loud'.

I work as a secretary in London and have a wide circle of friends whom I love, but they insist on using me as their own personal secretarial service, from booking restaurants to

sending them email addresses. How can I politely ask them to stop?

I am sure you have brought this upon yourself as nobody would ask you unless you were able to secure the difficult reservations they cannot get. So you have a choice: stop showing off your connections or stop complaining. Whenever I cannot get a table at a restaurant, I just ring up and make up some important name. I then pretend to be the security needing to do a recce, which never fails to fluster the people at reservations, whose lives are dazzled by the prospect of celebrities. On the night, you go straight to the table and order a drink and then signal for the manager. Most importantly, you look around sheepishly and whisper to him, in close earshot, that the VIP has caught something nasty like diarrhoea and is now indisposed to attend.

Can you assist me on the correct facial expression and body language that I must exude when bumping into my oldest married friend brazenly sashaying into a mutual friend's drawing room with his current *maîtresse*?

You should screw up neither your face nor your body. Indeed, you must show no sign of concern or envy. Your aloofness and contempt should be the unequivocal message. We men get particularly annoyed when our smoothness, apparent or otherwise, is not noticed. But if you cannot resist throwing your old friend a facial expression, then drop your eyebrows and squint your eyes, grit your teeth and protrude your lips, and grimace as vindictively as the Reverend Edward Casaubon in *Middlemarch*.

Is it ever permitted to comment on a friend's poor driving, and, if so, how should comments be approached? I'm

thinking of friends with whom I often drive down to the country, who, for example, hog the central lane on the motorway at slow speed, oblivious to the flashing lights and annoyance of the drivers behind them.

Once a year, Jimmy Goldsmith used to drive me from his home in Paris to his restaurant in the Bois de Boulogne, and we always had to go round the Arc de Triomphe. He drove very slowly, talking all the time, and never seemed to be in control, and all the cars around us would be honking and screeching to avoid near-misses. It was open season for road-rage. I used to be very nervous and petrified, not knowing whether to listen to his conversation or to tell him that he was the worst driver in the world. Yet we always made it safely out of the treacherous roundabout. Soon, I discovered that I rather enjoyed getting my adrenaline going, with the paradox of the excitement deriving from slow speed rather than fast speed. So you might resist being a back-seat driver, and simply enjoy yourself with nervousness and excitement.

· · ·

I notice lately that you have been bothered with some quite stupid questions. Please tell me how you are coping with that.

I would say in exactly the same way as I am coping with you, to wit, with aloofness and contempt. Don't worry about me. You look after yourself.

HOUSE GUESTS

'How does one tactfully suggest one's host turns
on the central heating?'

I N HONG KONG and China, where there are no country houses, still less estates, house guests are a rare breed. Indeed, all over Asia, where the well-off always live as urbanites, house guests are also few and far between. But of course in the West, and certainly in Britain, house guests abound, especially at the weekends or during holidays, and they move like busy migrants with their suitcases. Sometimes they even leave with heavier suitcases. It is very much a way of life, and no country house is without a spare bedroom or two, as they exist as a necessity to accommodate staying guests.

The grander houses with vast estates are of course often staffed to the hilt, although equally there are many examples of owners having fallen on hard times, and having to manage crumbling structures of rotten roofs and ceilings, and walls with rising damp, and consequently cold and draughty rooms, surrounded by burst sofas and unlaundered linens. When one stays at these distressed places, one has to be accompanied by humour or charity, or preferably a combination of the two: humour in order to make the experience into a practical joke for one's enjoyment, and charity in order to provide comfort to someone lonely and hard up.

I am not in possession of a country house in England, but I tend to take quite a number of shooting days and so effectively I have staying guests all the time. But on such occasions, because we shoot all day, my guests don't really require much looking after. All I have to do is to make sure that there are seven other comfortable beds and bathrooms, and that we are all served a hearty breakfast and a good dinner with vino, and most of all a decent lunch that should always be better than a perfunctory pie or stew. For shooting, it is also important to ensure that loaders are provided and that guns are placed with a good distribution of the better pegs.

Otherwise, I have house guests during the holidays when I take a boat or a house for a week or so. To all of them, I say only one thing: I will tell them what I will be doing and how I will be organizing each day, and they can each elect to fall in or not to fall in. If they can give notice of what they plan to do, all the better, but I don't really mind last-minute or even reversed decisions. This laissez-faire approach satisfies completely the whole point of being a host, to wit, to give maximum enjoyment to the guests. A host should not think about himself, but only about his guests – otherwise he should not have invited them. I dare say a lot of people will disagree with this level of altruism on the part of the host. But to my mind one would not be a host if not for one's guests, and so they should be the sole focus of one's attention.

But how about misbehaving guests? Guests who take advantage of the host's generosity? My view is that they will not be asked again and, on occasions, I might suggest seeking quiet revenge by, say, smuggling into their departing luggage a dead insect or animal. That said, the real secret is, of course, choosing the right house guests *ab initio*. There should always be one or two exceptional or remarkable people – interesting or beautiful people – from whom others will learn new and wonderful things. Authors, travellers and scientists are always good. And someone who can do magic – that's always entertaining. But, above all, it is essential that each of your guests has a good sense of humour, and is preferably witty as well, for the whole point of any holiday or leisurely gathering is to laugh. And to laugh out loud. So, make sure all your house guests are amusing people. Otherwise, don't ask them to anything or anywhere.

DIFFICULT SITUATIONS – GUESTS

What is the form when arriving at a friend's house where the butler greets one with a kiss on both cheeks? I do not know him socially and find his intimacy rather alarming.

It is obvious that either the butler is not a proper butler or you are uncontrollably attractive. I was once sent to call on the Prince of Hanover, and when I shook his hand after he opened the door, he said: 'I am the butler, and will tell His Royal Highness that you are here.' It also reminds me of when I was lunching with the late entrepreneur Mark Birley at Harry's Bar, and he said to me disdainfully about his new manager: 'If I see him kiss another woman, I am going to kill him.'

If one has the misfortune of breaking something that is clearly priceless and irreplaceable while staying with friends, what is the best way to deal with the situation?

You must immediately ask the host: 'What do you think?' You must gauge their reaction. If they say 'You must pay for it', then you must ascertain how much. If you can afford it, then you pay. If you can't afford it, then you must offer an instalment plan as an indirect plea for impecuniousness. If they say 'Never mind', then you should speedily accept their graciousness (lest they change their mind) and say something like: 'I'll make it up to you.' Then you must think of sending them whatever you can best afford with a grovelling note. If the object is sentimentally irreplaceable, then you might instantly kneel down in supplication and bow your head in contrition. This is bound to disarm your host and they are more likely than not to say: 'Please, please, get up – it doesn't matter at all.' Then, as before, you seize on their forgiveness straightaway before they change their mind.

When invited to stay with friends, is it wrong to ask for one's usual room? As a single elderly woman I prefer to sleep in a double bed. My friends have told me that for my forthcoming holiday weekend in southern Provence my usual room will be given to a young couple in their 20s and I will be stuck in a child's single bed.

If you have already been told that you are staying in a single bed, then there is no need for you to ask. It all depends on how well you know your host. If you are really great friends, you can then appeal for a possible upgrade. And if you don't know your host well enough, then it is rude to ask for something else, as it will be presumptuous. But you can always cancel if you think your accommodation is beneath you, although you should make sure that you have a better invitation. Otherwise, you might stew in your own unoccupied double bed over your holidays.

What is the form while staying with people for the weekend (or worse, longer) when one has to share a bathroom?

Go against the instinct that you should get to the bathroom before everybody else. It is much wiser to go afterwards, because if you went before, you would be obliged, out of sheer courtesy, to clean up before the next person; whereas if you were to go afterwards, you would expect the place to have been cleaned up by your predecessor, and you don't have to worry about cleaning up afterwards. The trick, however, is to make sure that you arrive with two new towels and a flannel, which you must remember to smuggle into your own bedroom before you go to bed. And always travel with a small room spray. My preference is a bottle of strong eucalyptus oil, which comes in very handy in any shared facilities. But in the final analysis, I simply wouldn't go and stay in any house where I have to share a bathroom with anyone, except perhaps Scarlett Johansson.

When it is late at night and one is staying with friends miles from the only shop and someone asks if they can smoke your last or second-last cigarette, what is an appropriate way of basically saying NO without appearing stand-offish? Unlike men, who always carry two cigars and seemingly happily hand out their spare to whomsoever wish it, we girls are reluctant to share the last of a pack . . .

Of course, the smart thing to do is not to concentrate on the cigarette being the last one but to see what distinct advantage you can gain by the circumstances of the request. Accordingly, if I were pulling and a very pretty girl came up to me and asked me for a cigarette, I would not only give her my last one but exaggerate the sacrifice in order to make an impression. Equally, if someone I do not like were to ask for my last cigarette, I would very conveniently be able to say to them, and sharply, that I wouldn't give them one if it was my last one! I once offered a cigar to a complete stranger in the depth of winter in Beijing, and this small gesture enabled me to ask him for a favour back some time later, and therefore I am always a champion of 'Androcles and the Lion'.

DIFFICULT SITUATIONS – HOSTS

As someone who lives in a pet-free house, I find it irritating when house guests arrive with their dogs and allow them to

treat my house as if it were their own – reupholstering the drawing room with dog hair, and worse crimes. How can I tactfully encourage them to leave their pets at home or in the car throughout their stay without causing offence?

If social-climbing, commercial networking or physical attraction were behind your invitation, then you must balance the acceptance of their pets against your readiness to suffer hair and what-have-you around your furniture and carpet. It then becomes a simple question of: 'Are you desperate enough to want them to come and tolerate their pets?' If you have no ulterior motive and it's a purely friendly invitation, then you should just tell your friends that you don't want them to come with their pets. Why should you not confess your preciousness to your friends? It's no worse than those irritating hosts who ask you to take off your shoes and walk barefoot on their light green Wilton carpet. Better to know before you arrive.

How would you advise me to ask my house guests to avoid wearing fake tan when they come to stay with me, as it stains my linen sheets?

I once met George Hamilton and confronted him with the question of which particular brand of fake tan he might recommend. He laughed and vehemently denied that he used any. I wish he were coming to stay with me, as I would then be able to find out from my white linen sheets if he was a liar or if I was colour-blind. On the assumption that you don't know George, you should use dark brown or black sheets, whose camouflage will enable you to use them both for normal people, as well as abnormal people with fake tan. It would of course be better for you not to have to invite any fake people. And best of all, for you not to have any friends with a fake tan. Thankfully, as a Chinese with a yellow complexion, I cannot use fake tan even if I wanted to, because I might go orange and be mistaken for a Martian.

What do you do when those who have accepted your invitation to holiday at your house, or to travel together as a group, suddenly cancel, especially at the last minute?

You do nothing, other than perhaps to wheeze in private irritation. If people cancel, let them cancel. The trick is not to get huffed up about the cancellation but see how the cancellation could work to your own advantage, such as having fewer people to look after or inviting somebody else who might be 'better'. Only the English get terribly upset about cancellations, because they plan and invite so far ahead, which somehow solemnizes acceptances into contractual promises. That's why foreigners don't like English invitations, because they want to be flexible. There are also cancellations we should definitely embrace without annoyance. I received acceptances to my 60th birthday celebration from five friends who effectively cancelled because they died before the day of my party.

I recently rented a holiday villa and invited some of my friends as guests. Two of them were repeatedly late for meals and, even worse, never made an effort to dress up properly for dinner. What should I have done to smarten up their act?

You should have done nothing and just let your guests enjoy themselves. It remains unfathomable to me that hosts should indulge in what they want rather than try to give pleasure to their guests. After all, that's the fundamental principle of entertainment. A stand-up comedian, say, would aim to make the entire audience laugh and if a couple of them were to leave in the middle, that's their choice. Hence if your 'misbehavin'' guests were enjoying themselves, you should simply let them be, especially on holiday.

Whenever I have guests staying, I always tell them to do whatever they feel like, and if they don't turn up to meals I am understanding personified. Or if they choose to stay in their rooms, that's also their business. This way, all the guests feel totally relaxed and the hosts will have fulfilled their job description.

I have old friends who are always encouraging me to invite them to my house in Provence. They like to be offered flexible dates and as much notice as possible. This year I invited them as long ago as January to stay in July. They replied that they were unable to come as they had other long-standing prior commitments (fishing in Iceland). Imagine, therefore, my surprise when I heard that the couple had subsequently accepted an invitation from a mutual friend to stay at his house in Provence during the same period; this house party will be glamorous. I am bound to bump into them there and need your advice on how to comport myself to avoid embarrassment.

No need to comport. Just choose to appear didactic or generous. If the former, you should shout out when you meet your friend that he is caught *in flagrante delicto* for abandoning your invitation for a better one, and is, therefore, a scallywag. Repeat loudly this accusation for maximum embarrassment. Alternatively, you can simply pretend that you had never invited him and just say a casual 'hello' to him in a very soft voice but immediately walk away and ignore him for the rest of the time. Such disdain, which could be interpreted as generosity, is bound to disarm your friend and make him feel doubly guilty.

COUNTRY WEEKENDS

As winter approaches I start to dread staying with friends at their draughty old houses in the country. Too often I find the log fires are ineffectual and the duvets wafer-thin. How do I tactfully suggest they turn on the central heating?

Arrive in some mountaineering gear with goggles, resembling Captain Scott, and say you are practising to go to the Antarctic and would prefer, for assimilation, to keep all your clothes on for drinks and dinner. If your feeling cold were still to go unnoticed, blow into your gloved hands, shake like a jelly in a high wind and remark that your friend's house provides perfect conditions for training. If you are not as daring as that, decline the invitation by citing hypothermia from the last visit.

Is it naff to bring gifts when you stay with your friends in their country houses? If not, what should they be? I don't want to appear rude or mean by not bringing anything. Also, what is the correct form for leaving on Sunday? I have noticed most guests leave before breakfast and the host has to guess how much food to prepare.

A gift should always be considered and not perfunctory like a box of chocolates or a bottle. Try to find something amusing so that your host could use it for future guests, with the bonus of saying: 'Oh, yes, it was so-and-so who brought it for me.' As for food, it's always necessary to have ample in the larder and the fridge with which to serve the maximum number of people for the maximum length of time. This is the only way to be a good host. A calculated host is not a good host.

I am the lucky recipient of weekend invitations to my friends' homes in the country – invariably from cottage to castle, I find the pillows in spare rooms rock hard. Is it acceptable for me to bring my own Hungarian goose feather pillows?

You must be incredibly spoilt. But if you really cannot sleep without your down pillows, then take one, but not two, as you don't need to be over-dramatic. And stop being obsessed by Hungary. Just as well you are not Chinese, as the traditional Chinese pillow was made with rock-hard porcelain, in which water was filled in order to cool or warm the nape. I must admit, however, that these are nowadays almost entirely used as door-stoppers.

What is the appropriate amount of money to leave as a tip in a large country house in England – as a single woman I usually leave £10 per night in my room.

Can you tell me what you can get for £10? More to the point, what can you get for £3.33 once your tenner has been split between the butler, the cook and the housemaid? The answer is nothing. Stop being so mean – or at least get someone not so parsimonious to sleep with you, so that he can, also on your behalf, leave, at least, what I call a 'Sir John Houblon' [his portrait appears on the back of a £50 note].

I live in a grand country house and invite people from all walks of life and all parts of the globe to stay. The family

visitors' book goes back many generations, and I have found to my horror lately guests writing more than just their name! How can I persuade them that a thank-you letter is the appropriate place to express one's thanks?

It is an ugly reflection on our world of commerce in which guests staying in hotels are encouraged to comment on their 'experiences', and most of them now confuse this invitation for mercantile entries with a simple signature in the family visitors' book. Ergo, if you wish to remain aloof about this traditional practice, you should stop inviting parvenus. I also abhor chocolate-box remarks, but don't mind witty one-liners like, as I once saw after a name, the marvellous words 'Quoth the raven!'

THANK-YOU GIFTS

When staying with friends for weekends I often choose to take along rather fabulous and not inexpensive soap from a shop in Elizabeth Street in Belgravia. So at a recent stay, I was rather horrified to find by accident in the chest of drawers in the corridor outside my room at least 10 years' supply of expensive soap from Elizabeth Street ... I felt rather hurt, to say the least. What should I do?

You have the choices of revenge or sufferance. If revenge, which is best served cold, you should scoop up all the bars you find in the chest of drawers, take them home and wait patiently before you are invited again, at which point you can bring with you all of the unused soaps BUT in some incredible packaging, which you must somehow get from Cartier or Hermès.

You should then smuggle the package into the bedroom of your host, and deposit it in a chest of drawers, so that its discovery is a surprise. This should embarrass your host, and stylishly so. If you, however, don't want to have all the bother, then you must put up and shut up, and don't take any more soap. Take something large which your host might not be able to bung into a chest of drawers. Maybe a paper kite?

Your episode reminds me of a lunch which the late Princess Diana gave my wife and me at her home in Kensington. There were just four of us, including a very young Prince Harry. During coffee, the Princess produced a rather smart bag from a famous brand and gave it to my wife, when an innocent but very observant prince remarked: 'Mummy, do you always give away presents others give you? How many more of those bags do you have?' We all looked at each other in a moment of stunned silence, then all of us burst out laughing. Nothing more was said and my wife took the bag, although it wasn't particularly nice and was never used, notwithstanding its glamorous provenance.

I have been invited to spend a Sunday at the holiday house of a former Portuguese business partner of my father, now a prominent politician. I wonder what I can possibly offer the man and his spouse, besides a flower bouquet, for showing my gratitude. Considering they are Portuguese, they must already have excellent local wines.

Portugal, arguably a country with the finest weather in the world, is curiously a bit of a holiday backwater. Recently, I was having a casual chat with an attractive croupier in between spins on the roulette wheel. She had been to the Algarve for a holiday and said that the weather could not have been more beautiful, yet she had been so bored that she said she and her boyfriend would never go back there again.

So your first question is whether you would have a boring holiday there; second, whether your father's business partner is going to be boring; and third, whether he would be bored by a boring present like a bouquet of flowers.

It is all rather sad for a country that was once mighty. I was very conscious of Portugal because I grew up in Hong Kong across from the shadow of the Portuguese colony of Macau. It was of course always a place famous for its gambling and pawn-shops, especially now, and for Dr Stanley Ho, the great Chinese casino magnate, who married a beautiful Portuguese woman as wife numero uno.

Also, when I was young and reading about amazing adventures, I was fascinated by what the Portuguese explorer Magellan did. Although he was attacked and killed during a fight in the Philippines during his stupendous journey westward around the globe, a small number of his crew did eventually make it back to their starting point in Seville, and so Magellan can be credited with organizing the first circumnavigation of the world.

If your father's friend is anyone worth his salt, he would enjoy discussing these questions with you rather than receiving any dubious token. But don't think just because Portugal produces fine wines that you can't impress him with, say, a bottle of 1935 port. I recently came across a description by a wine snob who said: 'Last year, I had the good fortune to drink a wine (port) from 1935 and, although it was delicate, it was still fresh and very much alive.' You must ask your politician friend how anything that had been bottled for 78 years could be 'fresh' and 'alive'.

I have taken up arriving to stay with people carrying an espresso machine (actually not a bad weekend house present – they only cost a little over £100). At the risk of appearing to mimic members of our royal family, I am increasingly inclined to travel with my own goods: pillows,

bedside radio, supplies of coffee and – dare I say it – my own soap. Am I becoming incredibly spoilt? Do you travel with essentials and if so, what are they?

When you start thinking that something is indispensable in your life, then it is time, I believe, that you should try to go without it. I often try to take myself out of my own comfort zone in case one day I am shipwrecked and have to fend for myself on a desert island. I want to be intelligent and practised in finding some ingenious way of managing without any of the things that might be considered necessary. An espresso machine is hardly necessary, especially taken with the disingenuous intent of giving it to your host when you really want to use it yourself. I also think that you must have *idées au-dessus de votre gare* by trying to emulate the grander members of the royal family. As for the soap, I think it will be your host who will worry about the one you leave behind, probably more than you worry about having your own when you arrive.

We will be visiting old friends over the summer holiday, which I am really looking forward to. Except for one thing: bad wine. They are of more modest means so their excellent cooking tends to be accompanied by wine of dismal quality. On a previous holiday we took turns shopping for food, which allowed me to buy a good bottle. It was recognized as expensive wine by our host, which resulted in a rather awkward situation for all of us. I am left with the choice of drinking bad wine or embarrassing our friends. What to do?

The answer couldn't be simpler: you send ahead, preferably a week or two before you arrive, one or two cases of the wine that you like, accompanied by a letter of advance gratitude for the invitation to stay. Therefore, the vino is ostensibly sent as a present to your host, from whom you should expect it to be served. But once I went overboard and dispatched in advance a case each of Corton-Charlemagne and Sassicaia, only to discover that the host held them back and served instead his usual inferior wines. So there's always the danger of dealing with a host who is a complete prat.

I am planning to take the book *Fifty Shades of Grey* as a house present to an upcoming hostess of mine whom I do not know particularly well. All my bridge-playing girlfriends are mad for it, but I have not read it except for page 148 – it seems rather lightweight to me. Do you have any views on chick lit?

This book by E. L. James has apparently become the first book to have sold a million copies on the internet. If only out of curiosity, I immediately bought a copy and started reading it. I was flabbergasted by its appalling prose! After 112 pages, the juicy bits that followed held as much titillation for me as a colony of elephant seals. Of course the reverse-snobs would say it's marvellous stuff and good on Ms James for making millions. But just remember nobody would really want to rate the Ikea catalogue, which has printed more copies than the Bible. Therefore, I would say E. L. James ought to be ashamed for bringing disrepute to the novel. What a difference the two initials of P.D. would have made to James! In my young days in the 1970s, everybody was raving and raging about John Fowles's *Daniel Martin*. I saw it everywhere in the streets, in bus shelters, in subways in Noo Yawk. That's proper lit. *Grey* is proper litter.

• • •

**David – I like you, in a completely non-sexual way. Is this an
acceptable feeling for a man? Kind regards, André**

Not if your name is André!

DINNER PARTIES

'Is it ever acceptable at a party secretly to swap place cards?'

I F I WERE TO SET a syllabus at a finishing school on dinner parties, I would simply prescribe the watching of two films: Luis Buñuel's *The Exterminating Angel*, and Blake Edwards's *The Party*, starring Peter Sellers. Once one has watched these two cinematic treasures, one cannot fail to realize how excruciatingly dull our own dinner parties are. In Buñuel's surrealistic masterpiece, following the final course of a lavish dinner party, the guests adjourn to the music room for a piano recital, after which each of them finds that they are somehow inexplicably compelled to stay in the room. Their mysterious psychological imprisonment in the room continues for many days, during which time one of the guests dies and a young couple commit suicide. Someone eventually manages to smash through a wall to access a water pipe, only for several sheep to find their way in, whereupon they are promptly slaughtered and roasted over a fire made from the floorboards of the room. Wouldn't this be the kind of dinner party everyone dreams of? If it does not sound the stuff of dreams to you, I can only take this as meaning that you are unimaginative, insular and unadventurous – all of which are the inferior characteristics of the bourgeoisie, for whom the dinner party represents the social summit of their jejune lives.

In *The Party*, in turn, Peter Sellers reminds us of the inanity of a fancy dinner party in Hollywood. He plays an unknown Indian actor who is fired from the film he has been working on after accidentally triggering an enormous explosion and destroying the whole set. But when the producer learns of this mishap and goes to write Sellers's name down as a reminder never to work with him again, he instead prolongs this unfortunate comedy of errors by accidentally adding the hapless actor's name to his wife's guest list for a dinner party.

Now, I'm quite sure that you can imagine the furore that would be caused by your arrival at a dinner to which you were not really invited, but where your name was nonetheless on the list and there was a place set for you at the table. And in true Sellers style, he ends up causing not so much a furore as an unholy ruckus, scattering bird seed all over the floor as he tries to feed a macaw bird in a huge cage, plunging his fist into a pail of caviar, and inadvertently impaling his main course on the tiara of a female guest on the opposite side of the table. How marvellous it would be to attend such a party!

And yet, more often than not, all the real dinner parties we go to are incredibly dull. I would say that was true of well over half of all the dinners that I have ever been to – and that's why I rarely go to dinner parties any more. Whenever I do find myself at a particularly pedestrian event, I inevitably find that I am prevented from leaving by convention and good manners, and so suffer tedium for the sake of politeness. I can't do it any more. Invitation to lunch, on the other hand, is something that I find much more attractive. Because it usually lasts only an hour and a half at most, the suffering coefficient is manageable.

The best solution, I find, is to give the dinner myself. Then I am in absolute control, and I will ensure the absence of droning bores and pretentious soufflés. The first secret is to cram everyone as close together as possible, preferably so that we can all hear each other, and to ensure an array of beautiful or very attractive guests (or if ugly, then exceedingly accomplished, at least). The visual starters are important. The second secret is to have intelligent and articulate guests. There is nothing more dispiriting than to have a dinner conversation that is unsubstantial, for it will descend into gossip and hearsay rubbish. And if you can't find a handful of these people, then don't give a dinner party.

GUEST LIST

I have been told by a friend that dinner parties are the height of bourgoisedom [*sic*]. As I am constantly left owing people for their hospitality to me, a dinner party at my flat is the only way I have of really paying them back. What sort of a dinner party displays the stamp of being bourgeois, and is it bad to be bourgeois?

It is bourgeois to fuss over any dinner party. It is also bourgeois to have the same people who know each other to dine together. To lift yourself further out of embourgeoisement, you should always dress up properly, but not require your guests to do so. And you should always have your best crockery and cutlery out, with a white tablecloth and large white linen or cotton napkins; and candles of course – black for chicness, and never red. Always limit your numbers to six or eight. The conversation must be grand enough to include history, politics and culture – and never gossip. And most important of all, the water you serve must be chilled. If you have got all of these ingredients, you can tell your friend to mind their own bourgeois business.

My husband and I enjoy entertaining in our home, hosting dinner parties of 10 to 12 people. We disagree on how to construct the guest list. I believe most of our friends to be interesting and outgoing, and therefore able to socialize and converse with anyone present. My husband prefers to put together a group that he feels share something in common. How do you and your wife select dinner party guests?

I dislike having one-dimensional guests. When they are more or less the same, they increase the chances of boring conversations. I much prefer a landscape of highs and lows. Always try to get people who you think will NOT get on, so that one can hear the different sides of their stories.

Maximize witticism and laughter, which, for me, is the most important point of gathering for dinner. Remember that anecdotes are preferable to jokes: it is a fine art to be able to recount a story with language that flows and titillates and exaggerates. By having all sorts of guests, we get to learn how others live differently from us. I'd love to know, for example, the extent of wife-swapping in prim suburbia; to know if these rumours I hear do actually take place behind those net curtains through which furtive faces peer. Fascinating!

When inviting guests to dine in one's own home, is it just me or is it quite rude of those one is inviting to quiz one about the guest list for the evening before they make their decision? I think it's frightful – what are your views?

Given the choice, I dare say you yourself would love to know the other guests before you decide to accept an invitation – and those of you who say it's 'frightful' are invariably frightful yourselves. We Chinese always have no qualms whatsoever on insisting to see the guest list before we accept, which is so sensible. But, of course, above the veneer of respectability in England, one is not supposed to ask. Yet we all live in fear of turning up to an event of either tedium or nauseum. At one dinner, I was reduced to telling the women on either side that I found their conversation 'totally resistible'. So I never accept any invitation from a host who is known to have invited a couple of bores. One is containable, two becomes infectious.

With largish dinner parties for, say, 30 or more, how does one cope with last-minute cancellations which invariably put out the *places à table*? And should one get furious with people who cancel at the last minute?

I have come to resign myself to the fact that nowadays there will always be five or six people who cancel at the last minute either because they are liars or half-liars or quarter-liars. People always say they have a cold or flu and do not wish to pass it on to me or my guests, which is a pathetic excuse. I hear this so often that I regard it as a white lie. Then there are all sorts of other excuses which are really irrelevant if they ain't coming. And it is extremely boring to have to juggle round the guests with cancellations. I once adopted the placement* simply in alphabetical order for a dinner for 90 people, believing that cancellations would become irrelevant. Amazingly, on that occasion, there wasn't a single cancellation. Mind you, it was a dinner I was giving for a 90-year-old man. So most of his guests were geriatrics. I am sure that they belonged to that dependable generation who don't cancel just because they feel a little chill coming on.

Worst of all, however, are those who at the last minute cancel a shoot which takes a great deal of organization, not to mention expense. Particularly annoying is if they regard mercantile emergencies as a sufficiently good excuse to cancel a mid-week shoot. There is clearly some truth in what I was brought up to believe – that gentlemen don't shoot at weekends!

My husband and I hosted a small dinner party for a couple for whom we even changed the original date to suit. On the night, they spent the entire time before dinner telling our

---

* Note from Ed. According to the late Sir Hardy Amies '*placement*' is what the French do with their money. He maintained that the correct phrase is '*place à table*'.

guests that they had 'double booked' and wouldn't stay for dinner or the entertainment. What is your advice on how to deal with them, as we have not spoken to them since?

You shouldn't get too upset about undependable guests. I deal with them all the time. If I got the kind of hernia you get every time someone cancels at the last minute, I would be paralysed for life already. The point about dinner parties is that you should become an excellent host and not worry too much about appalling guests. If you don't like any of them, simply don't invite them. They will be the ones who get annoyed if your invitations are worth their salt. Aloofness is by far the best weapon against bad manners.

A dear friend of mine – very charismatic, generous to a fault and hospitable too – is a serial jacker of invitations. He initially accepts with alacrity and then inevitably a couple of days later rings and says: 'Oh darling, so sorry, cannot come', leaving my guest list rather compromised. What is the cut-off point for re-inviting guests with such an affliction?

I have always noticed how meticulous the English are about invitations, and how dinners are arranged weeks in advance, with a great deal of fuss over the cut of the beef or the exact number of chops required, and agony over the *place à table*. Then there would be arms thrown up in alarm when someone chucks. All of this is, of course, totally alien to the East – we Chinese, plus the Indians, Arabs and Russians, are more cavalier about invitations, and do not really operate properly on RSVPs. So my advice is to be relaxed about cancellations, especially if you are anxious to show off your gallery guest. If he genuinely cannot come, there is nothing you can do. And if he were to contrive some excuse not to come, then he doesn't really want to, in which case, do you really want him? A magnet can be both attractive and repellent!

SEATING PLAN

Do you think it acceptable for an Italian guest at a party secretly to swap place cards, when these cards have been arranged with great care by the hostess to give guests the opportunity of meeting someone she thinks they will enjoy the company of, and with whom they have shared interests, so they can sit next to their friends?

As the host, you would understandably be upset if any of your guests were to change your place at table – nothing more irritating than a busybody interfering with your own arrangement, especially if you yourself had spent time agonizing over all the names for a big party. But as the guest, you might feel a sense of panic and a necessity to change from being placed next to somebody you don't want to sit next to. Italians are always predictable for making a beeline for pretty girls, and will juggle place cards. But for others, there could be genuine reasons for displacement, ranging from halitosis to a long-standing feud. John Aspinall gave a dinner once, and was furious with Jemima Goldsmith for swapping her place card, although it struck me as rather hypocritical of him, as he went round in a macho way deriding middle-class values – and you don't get more middle class than being antsy about placement. But I was very happy on that occasion because I was the beneficiary of Goldsmith's adjacency, not that I was the reason for her swap, but rather that she hated the prospect of sitting in between her flankers who were designated by Aspinall.

I would also act in an emergency, as I did once, on discovering that I was to be wedged among an entire table of crashing bores.

Surreptitiously, I slipped the place card into my pocket and asked the waiter, with a little tip, to dispose of my cutlery, crockery, glasses, napkin and, vitally, my chair, before furtively leaving through the back door. It was a social sleight of hand worthy of the *Marie Celeste*.

Recently, I attended a dinner at which, to everyone's surprise, the seating plan was done strictly in alphabetical order. The result was not entirely satisfactory, as many people seemed to complain, including two people who were arch-enemies made to sit adjacent to each other.

I think using the alphabetical order for *place à table* is an eminently scientific method of proving the vacuity of large dinners. It demonstrates the point, which I have long suspected, that in any gathered crowd, most of the people dislike most of the others. So why bother bringing everyone together? I abhor sitting between people I don't know; or those whom I half know and don't want to know more; or, even worse, those I know well and really can't stand. So I hope the alphabetical order will become fashionable, or even de rigueur, so that people think twice before accepting such invitations, knowing they will probably sit next to the same people again and again, or even for ever.

I recently gave a dinner party for a friend. Placement was as ever absolutely key to the whole evening but on arrival a guest changed her placement openly and while sucking a lemon – because she 'did not want to sit next to X as he has nothing to talk about'. Thus we had a husband and wife sitting next to one another. Should I have objected more vociferously than I did?

I don't at all mind having couples sit together, because one doesn't have to make an effort with one's own spouse or lover or partner. This practice also reduces the probability of being sandwiched between two bores – the curse of any dinner party. But I can understand your irritation from seeing one of your guests openly changing her place at table. The effrontery is not so much the fastidiousness of your guest, but rather the direct implication that you have got things wrong – or, worse still, have tedious guests. Hurting the vanity of the host is not the proper behaviour of a guest. I am, however, considerably more relaxed than you, because at any of my lunches or dinners, I don't really care where people sit as long as they are happy – after all, isn't that the aim of all entertainment? Mind you, I am rather an intolerant guest, and if I see boring types looming as my neighbours, I prepare myself to be obnoxious and on one or two occasions have disdainfully uttered to the bores: 'I must tell you that I find your conversation totally resistible.' At other times, I sham having lost my voice so that I don't have to talk at all. But it is important that one acts this out properly, perhaps by quietly hawking a few times or contriving a few throat coughs.

Recently, I attended a dinner on the morning of which I received the following email: 'Just to say, we have you confirmed to join us for what should feel like an intimate dinner. The dinner is seated. A seating plan for this group is a wonderful 3D puzzle. It can work beautifully but if someone just decides not to turn up no amount of brain cycles can solve for that. So if you have now changed your plans and can no longer join, we need to know ASAP. No one likes a lonely seat next to them ... And – a friendly heads up – unless justified, last-minute cancellations aren't

ideal . . . we have an elephant's memory for those who do cancel on us or worse, just don't show up . . .' What do you think?

I think it is a missive I'd love sending out but wouldn't. Far too didactic for a private affair. This was obviously a corporate event, and although rather belligerent, is essentially right, at least for the English, who fuss a great deal over placement. It won't, however, cut much ice in Asia. Manners are relative. An open belch is often a compliment to the chef in certain countries, while it is obviously regarded as rude in Britain, except perhaps among pot-bellied darts players in pubs.

ALCOHOL

I often find at parties or dinner that the champagne is flat. Is it all right to mention this to the host?

You must contrive an early excuse to make a toast to your host by pouring two glasses from the same flat bottle. Then make sure you clink the glasses and sip together, looking at each other's eyes. At that precise moment, raise one of your eyebrows and move your lips sideways slightly and direct a faintly surprised gaze at your glass, tilting it gently towards your host. Unless your host is completely stupid, the flatness of the bubbles will be indubitably registered and, one hopes, rectified.

I was invited to dinner by a long-time work acquaintance, and duly brought a nice bottle of wine (1985 Margaux, no less). When I arrived at his home, I discovered not only that he himself was teetotal but his other guests also took a dim view of alcohol consumption. With my gift consigned to

the kitchen counter, I sat forlornly through an achingly sober evening. Would I have been impolite to insist on a glass of wine?

First of all, it is inconsiderate to bring one bottle of wine to a dinner party. It's never enough. Always bring a brace. We Chinese say: 'All good things come in pairs.' Second, always do some proper homework on acquaintances as hosts. Being cavalier about a suitable present is shoddy manners. Equally bad is asking for a glass of wine in your circumstances, as that would have been too obvious a suggestion of drinking from your own bottle that you had brought as a present. But if you had fiendishly brought a claret of the 1981 or 1983 vintage, known for their fading bouquet, your suggestion of drinking it sooner rather than later might prompt the host to say: 'Let's drink it now!'

Whose wine does one drink when hosting a dinner party: either the wine you as host have chosen (and possibly decanted) or that which your guests bring?

Of course one drinks what one serves as host. Generally no decanting except in two circumstances: first, if your dining room is sufficiently grand and there is a fair bit of silver on the table and everyone is being served; or, second, if one is serving plonk, in which case decanters could be used as decoys for the plonkiness of the vino. Never drink what is brought. This is because using a bottle of wine from one guest, or different bottles of wine from several guests, would mean guests drinking different wines, which would not only be confusing but also unfair if there is a qualitative differential between the bottles.

Of course young people, who are more used to 'bring-a-bottle' parties, should just drink whatever they can lay their hands on, and I doubt any of them would even think about using a decanter. At the other end of the scale, we have wine snobs, or what I call wine bores. They often set a bad example by pontificating about vintages and using words like 'bouquet' or 'timbre' and recounting, tediously, their visits to exotic châteaux. I have always liked the short story by Roald Dahl in which a wine snob arrogantly claims to know, simply from sniffing and gurgling, exactly what wine is being served in the decanters, until the moment the butler comes into the dining room with the snob's spectacles, which he had inadvertently left in the library, having used them to read the labels of the bottles that had been emptied and decanted. How I wish such an exposé would occur more often.

Using a decanter has nothing to do with being a toff. It has two practical uses. First, it enables the drinker to separate the liquid from the sediment. Nothing worse than getting a mouthful of dregs right at the end of the bottle. Second, it introduces air to the wine, allowing it to open up fully. How else could you appreciate notes of burnt toast, tobacco box and damp horse saddle?

Here we go again, a wine bore evoking 'notes of burnt toast, tobacco box and damp horse saddle'! How on earth can you justify the aroma of a damp horse saddle? [*Readers can make jokes too – Ed.*]

Of course we all know about sediments and airing. But you don't need a decanter with which to manage these issues. You could simply uncork a bottle with minimal movement and let the wine breathe through its natural spout and pour carefully, avoiding the bottom deposits. On the contrary, when pompous sommeliers decant, they often unwittingly shake up all the sediment in a bottle and, in fact, make it worse by decanting.

Of course it is perfectly acceptable to have bottles on the dining table, as long as they are placed in a wine coaster, preferably silver, silver plate or tole, with the practical purpose of preventing a water stain from condensation on a chilled bottle, or red wine dribbling from the neck and staining the mahogany. And who would not wish to share with their guests the decorative excellence of a bottle from Château Mouton Rothschild for example?

I disagree. Coasters don't really work with chilled wines as the condensation is never altogether collected at the base, which is always made of silver or even grooved wood which doesn't absorb water, so that when the bottle is lifted to replenish a glass, it always drips. As for red wines, why worry about the occasional small drips? If you eat with a tablecloth, which is always the best, the stain won't matter. And so what if it stains the mahogany table? Shouldn't the table suit us, rather than us having to suit the table? There might be an argument about a precious piece of Chippendale, say, but even then, why use anything valuable and worry endlessly about preserving its resale value? But you are absolutely correct in observing the clever labelling on all bottles of Château Mouton Rothschild. Baron Philippe came up with the brilliant idea in 1924 of commissioning artists to draw original labels for their bottles. They included Picasso, Braque, Chagall, Miró, Dalí, Balthus, Bacon and Koons. So you are right, plenty to talk about, although it assumes that one is being served a Mouton Rothschild.

Your recent revelation that you are a teetotaller has me wondering whether you have a preprandial routine to help you cross the threshold from work to personal time. Many who sip wine and other libations before dinner do so as

part of a daily ritual to help them wind down. How do you do that?

When I come home from a hard day's work, I open the door and my wife is standing there in front of me, smiling, giving me a kiss and taking from me my briefcase. She locks arms with me and puts me in a comfortable armchair and, kneeling down, changes my shoes into slippers. She then gives me a cold flannel and pours me a cold drink and asks me when I would like dinner. She goes upstairs and runs a bath for me and waits to take away my laundry.

This is, of course, my fantasy of how I wouldn't mind being unwound at the end of a hard day. In truth, nothing of the sort happens and I just go home and fling my shoes off and get a cold fizzy drink and sit down with my dogs. The begum is always doing something else. Sometimes I try to irritate her with music by Olivier Messiaen or Peter Maxwell Davies, whose dissonances I know annoy her. Just as she would be irritated if I lit up a Cuban cigar, say a Punch Double Corona cut into two equal halves, with the lower half smoked first. At this point, my wife would be wound up and I would not be winding down. Maybe you are right that those of us who are teetotal, as my wife is also, seem to miss out on being properly relaxed by alcohol.

CONVERSATION

What does one do round a dinner table at which the conversation is too intellectual for one to understand and participate in?

You should either blame yourself for being ignorant or your fellow diners for being insensitive. A good host would always bring everyone into the conversation and, given the opportunity, you should initiate topics about which you know at least a little. They just have to be interesting. I once had a fascinating conversation with a street shoe-shiner. I bought him a bowl of noodles and he told me all about the secret of spit-polishing shoes. He explained that the best shine came from the reflection of light over a smooth surface and not letting any of it be captured within the thousands of pores that are found in the leather. Therefore, it is necessary to rub polish into the leather endlessly in order to fill all the tiny holes. This goes to show that even someone engaged in what might seem a lowly and mundane job could, nonetheless, be alluringly intellectual and erudite.

Is it acceptable to introduce conundrums at dinner parties? Can they be a substitute for good conversations? Are they boring? Is one a bore for introducing them? Presumably they are better during the holiday season when people are more relaxed?

Conundrums are indeed better dispensed during the holiday period. But off season, they ought to be avoided as not everyone likes solving puzzles, and conundrums divide the table up into those who have brains and those who don't, at least superficially. Generally, however, there are many boring conundrums, usually introduced by bores, who think themselves clever for knowing the answers. But there are some very good ones that are far from boring and I love them as elegant puzzles. They are also useful weapons against those who are arrogant or conceited. It is satisfying to watch them failing to come up with the solutions and looking a bit stupid.

At a shooting dinner recently, I threw down the gauntlet with the following couple of very clever conundrums:

(1) Three friends decided to go out to dinner and agreed to split the bill, which came to £30. So each person paid £10. But when the waiter took the money to the cashier he was told there had been a mistake and that the bill was only £25. So the waiter was told to return £5 to the diners. But the cunning waiter thought this would be awkward because three into £5 won't go. Therefore he decided to pocket £2 for himself and returned only £3. Accordingly, each diner was given a £1 refund. This means each of them had paid £9, or £27 in total, because three times £9 is £27. Add the £2 the waiter had pocketed and it adds up to only £29. Where is the missing £1?

(2) A clever boy decided to go fishing with a rod measuring 5ft long. He wanted to travel by bus but at the bus stop the conductor told him that the policy of the bus company was not to allow on board any object more than 4ft long, other than the passengers. The boy then did something to his fishing rod, and the conductor was happy to allow him on board with the 5ft rod. Why this sudden change of mind? What did the boy do to persuade the conductor to let him on with his rod? The answer is not a silly one. On the contrary, it consists of the cleverest answer to a conundrum that I know of. (The boy doesn't retract the rod, or bend it, or stick any part of it out of the window, or do anything silly.)

I have received a lot of mail from readers about the two conundrums I set out recently. Some offered solutions, most of which were wrong, and most begged for the answers. So I will, at least, reveal the solution to one of them, but not for the missing-pound conundrum, which is really too good to expose. It has driven people completely mad. I have had telephone calls in the middle of the night from friends offering me their solutions. But when I ruffle them with counter observations, they hang up in desperation. For such a good conundrum, much like a wonderful magic trick by Dynamo or Derren Brown, I think it is not right to let the cat out of the bag. Therefore, I am going to leave the missing-pound conundrum intact and say no more on the matter.

I am, however, happy to offer the solution to the riddle of the schoolboy angler who wanted to get on a bus with a 5ft-long fishing rod but was told he could not take on board any object more than 4ft in length.

What he did was to find a thin box measuring 3ft by 4ft. He then placed the 5ft-long fishing rod across the diagonal of the box. This would fit in because of Pythagoras' theorem on right-angled triangles: the square of the hypotenuse (the side opposite the right angle) is equal to the sum of the squares of the other two sides. It is the classic 3, 4, 5 right-angled triangle. This way, the boy fulfils the bus regulation limiting all objects carried on board to 4ft or less. QED.

Now, an easy conundrum to restore your confidence: how far can a monkey run into the forest?

I recently hosted a shooting dinner at which my guests became rather ebullient, probably because of plenty of claret; and, one after another, began to gang up on me, disagreeing with everything I said as we debated on the subjects of ethnic prejudices and moral turpitude. Soon the whole argument round the table turned into a shouting match, and I was completely left alone, abused and under siege. My question is: what does a host do with rude guests?

There is rudeness, and there is rudeness. The first kind, which is good, consists of banter among good friends; whereas the second kind, which is bad, consists of what might be regarded as malice aforethought, the ingredient for murder. I suspect that if you were gathered for a shooting party, then you would be among good friends, unless it was for a corporate event, in which case, it deserves a shouting match. My conclusion is that it is much more fun and amusing to be arguing among friends.

Remember that phantasmagorical film by the genius Luis Buñuel, *The Exterminating Angel*, in which people argued fiercely around the table, but were somehow prevented from leaving the dining room? That is the ultimate for any decent dinner party. The fact that you might be host should be an irrelevance, because if you have a sense of style, you should not feel that a host should be any more or less rude than your guests. In an argument, you must always hold your own, and if you can't, then shut up. As they say: 'If you can't stand the heat, get out of the kitchen.' But next time, if you are expecting your guests to be belligerent, then do what I once did by hiding beforehand a megaphone under the dining table by your seat. And as the crescendo of the argument reaches its climax, execute an ambush by producing the megaphone and just shout down it your arguments as loud as possible, turning on its volume setting to maximum, thereby drowning out everyone else. The effect never fails to bring you a Napoleonic sense of triumph – and considerable laughter with admiration!

What do you do if you were host at a dinner at which your guests start arguing with each other? Do you let them fight or do you intercede and try to make peace? Would you react differently if your guests were eminent people and you selfishly wished to hear them?

The best thing to do is allow your guests to carry on arguing. I always like some firm disagreements over the dinner table to liven up the food and beverage, or some interesting anecdotes, which, if told with proper embellishments, are far superior to jokes. I once had Freddie Ayer, the brilliant philosopher, and Roald Dahl, the great children's writer, come for dinner. They both boasted about their squeezes like a game of call-my-bluff. To claim decisive victory, at least in quality, Dahl told a story about sleeping one night in the bunker of the Dorchester hotel, and how he saw Ernest Hemingway two beds away, separated by a woman in between them. Of course what Dahl recalled from that night might well have been one of his vintage *Tales of the Unexpected*. I simply couldn't tell. Ayer, arguably the world's most authoritative empiricist by virtue of his logical positivism, was naturally sceptical about Dahl's anecdote. But for me, the two fossils bantering for the higher status of virility was faintly sad but also quaint. That's the kind of dinner I like.

ENTERTAINMENT

What sort of music, if any, should be played for a dinner party at home? Should restaurants also play background music?

For atmosphere, background music at home when guests begin to arrive for dinner is just about acceptable – although ghastly bijou pieces by the likes of Kenny G and Richard Clayderman should be banned at all costs. Cole Porter, Nat King Cole or Ella Fitzgerald are OK because their lyrics and melodies have sub-stance, and their mood of a golden age often adds to the general atmosphere. Somehow, for me, classical music doesn't work as well as background music. Bach or Chopin always sound contrived because they are more hackneyed than erudite. Anything symphonic is bound to be a bit heavy. And operatic extracts, particularly from The Three Tenors, and particularly, particularly Nessun Flipping Dorma, are simply unacceptable.

Of course all music should be switched off during dinner. Common sense dictates that conversations should properly anchor a decent dinner without any distractions. But nowadays the intrusion is much more likely to come from the silent uses of the iPhone or BlackBerry under the table, rather than any music in the background. Indeed, in restaurants, the sad sight of diners using their mobiles is making any background music irrelevant. My trick is to email my guests – or hosts – round the same table with messages like 'Are you going to continue looking at your screen, ignoring us and spoiling a fairly civilized dinner?', which have become a template on my BlackBerry.

I love performances before or after dinner. Recently, I was staying at Houghton Hall, Norfolk, admiring its extraordinary exhibition of pictures, which had once been sold off to Catherine the Great but some of them borrowed back to be put *in situ*. Luckily for all of us, a concert pianist and our host played both before and after dinner on a piano that had been a present to Lady Cholmondeley from Rubinstein. It was a joy listening to Rachmaninov and Schumann and that divine transcription of Gluck's *Orfeo ed Euridice*. All a bit old-fashioned, some might argue, but these musical interludes make us appreciate the enhancement of music.

Most of all, I miss those wonderful bands in black tie with glamorous singers at restaurants and nightclubs. I would love to see the return of the kinds of burlesques that used to make places like Berlin alluring and magical. We don't listen enough and we don't spend enough time listening.

Don't you get tired of hosts who insist, particularly before one sits down for dinner, on a tour of their house? Is it acceptable to prescribe a tour of one's own home?

No, never prescribe a tour of one's home. It's too keen to show off and a bit gauche. But if your guests specifically ask to see your house, you can decide to show them with nonchalance. Cliff Richard once invited a few of us who were staying in an adjacent villa in Barbados to go over to his garden for cocktails. He then explained that the *QE2* would soon come round the headland and when it is steaming right in front of the house, the liner would shut off all her lights and bring them on and then shut them again – as a sign of salute!

Sure enough, the *QE2* came round and when it was against the horizon in front of us, all her lights, on a wave of Cliff's command, blinked three times like a giant Morse code transmitter. It was very impressive. Cliff Richard had taken the 'home tour' to new heights. How did he do it? He had made a prior arrangement with the captain of the boat and used a torch-light on his balcony as a cue. The even cleverer part of the trick is that we could almost hear the captain on the boat boasting to his passengers that when the lights of the ship go on and off, Cliff Richard in his villa would acknowledge them with flashes of light from his home.

SERVING

When entertaining at home, is it more polite and elegant to serve the ladies round the table before the men? Is it also acceptable to serve the food already on the plate? Is it considered pompous nowadays to make people wear black tie for a dinner party?

Serving the ladies first smacks of antimacassars. The practice is often considered, pretentiously and erroneously, to be 'the proper thing to do'. It also takes longer for the food to go round, making it cold. It irritates me, as a man, to see all that food criss-crossing before my eyes with untouchability. I spot a particularly well-charred chop, only to see it snatched by someone else before I take my turn. Besides, in an age of equality, I am sure feminists would not expect to be treated as the superior gender in a queue for grub. At any dinner I give, I am served first, along with the person opposite me, and we go round clockwise and anti-clockwise with understated haste and everyone is expected to start as soon as the food lands on their plate. Second, plated food is definitely not for me. The format belongs to refectories at schools or monasteries, commercial restaurants, or corporate social functions. It's silly to apportion everyone the same of each part of a dish. We should be able to exercise personal preference and take more meat or less veg, or vice versa. As for black tie, the trouble is that there will always be the egalitarian or someone with a jacket potato on their shoulder refusing to wear one, thereby spoiling the whole visual effect.

My wife and I disagree about the convenience of waiting for all to have been served the second course of a meal before starting. While I don't feel comfortable beginning the second course when there is still somebody with an empty dish, my wife prefers to ask the convivium to start eating. Do you think that the correct procedure depends on the number of people around the table, as she says?

Unless the Queen is present, one should always start without waiting. This is only sensible because otherwise the food will get cold. Even if what is served is cold, it just seems rather superfluously middle class for everyone to wait before tucking in. It's like saying that we should not behave like schoolchildren eating in a refectory at a boarding school. But that's exactly how we should behave – never losing our juvenility. It also takes the pomposity out of dining. Whenever I am host, I am always served first, and I always start eating first so that others can follow – and I tell them to. But of course I would have to change this selfish habit if Her Majesty were ever to come to a luncheon or dinner.

Having yourself served first at dinners that you are hosting reverses accepted mores – and your 'follow me' justification seems weak. Doesn't it generate many uncomfortable moments?

'Accepted mores'? We are only talking about having dinners, hardly an ethical issue. And why should my setting the example of eating immediately be 'weak'? On the contrary, it sends a strong cue to all my guests to start eating without waiting. This practice makes everyone far from uncomfortable but relieved! Furthermore, it allows the serving of second helpings to be staggered so that the maximum number of diners is eating at any one time. Try it out yourself before you castigate a perfectly sensible routine that should rightly supersede a silly one that only makes food go cold.

I agree on starting the eating procedure, but I am a bit surprised by your statement that when you are the host, you are served first. Shouldn't you be served last as the host?

Not at all. Tasting the food first gives me the opportunity to ascertain that what is being served is good enough. Now and then I have had to send food back because it was not hot enough, which is my bête noire; once, I found a rather nasty strand of hair in spaghetti cooked in the octopuses' own ink! In imperial China, food served for the emperor and empress was always tasted first by a servant, often a eunuch in the Qing dynasty, to prove the absence of poison, which would have turned the silver chopsticks black (although this would not happen with polonium), or caused the unfortunate taster to keel over.

EMERGENCIES

What is the protocol if somebody were to be taken suddenly ill round a dinner table? Obviously one would have to attend to the patient. But overall, should one then simply carry on stoically or make a big fuss and call an early end to the dinner?

Sangfroid, although a French word, is one of the English characteristics I most admire. So I'd say, generally, carry on as if nothing has happened. I was once at a dinner in the middle of which a peer of the realm suddenly collapsed with a heart attack. There was a moment of absolute panic. Having mastered first aid as part of my Duke of Edinburgh's Award while at school, I went straight over to give the old man mouth-to-mouth resuscitation. It was not a pleasant experience, but I managed to revive him – and took him back to his home round the corner, telling the host to carry on. A week later, the surviving peer wrote to me and thanked me for saving his life. He offered me tea at his home. I replied by asking him what I would have to do to get lunch.

What does one do when an extra guest turns up for a sit-down dinner, either because of an admin error or through another guest bringing along someone extra?

Once Sir Philip Green and Richard Caring asked me to bring 'Boris' to dinner, when they meant Boris Johnson, and I genuinely thought they meant Boris Berezovsky. On the night I was late, and a short bald Russian oligarch, instead of a spiky-haired tall Caucasian, turned up at Sir Philip's pad. To give him his due, he welcomed his surprise guest, possibly because of the two rather burly bodyguards in tow. By the time I arrived, we had realized the comedy of errors for which Evelyn Waugh could not have written a better *Scoop* if he had tried! We dined together as if nothing had happened, even if I glimpsed a few contorted faces from my hosts. But full marks to them for playing the entire pantomime out with real style.

The climax of the evening came when I eventually took Berezovsky off the premises, who then asked me: 'Who were those two people?' Green was heard laughing aloud for a whole day afterwards. I did produce Boris Johnson at a subsequent dinner. Needless to say, we all chuckled non-stop. The exemplary lesson from Green is to keep calm, and just improvise on the cameo surprise. The trick is to achieve accommodation as an acrobatic host and not to become a whinger who doesn't rise to the social challenge.

KNOWING WHEN TO LEAVE

What does one do when a dinner, especially a large function, drags on and on without the end in sight, and everyone is bored and tired but finds it slightly awkward leaving 'early'?

People always talk about guests being rude. But I always ask the question of when a host is rude. The answer must be when the host is being inconsiderate. And it is inconsiderate to incarcerate one's guests. It's known as false imprisonment. Whenever I notice that it is getting rather late and the pudding has still not come, I become irate. I used to be embarrassed about leaving, but now I simply get up and leave – the trick is not to make any fuss and say no goodbyes.

At any large gathering nobody would notice, and if it is a dinner party I would bet that others would want to leave as well. It's time for guests to show up selfish hosts who believe that they have the right to bag the presence of their guests interminably. They don't.

How can (elderly) early birds deal with hosts who are night owls regarding dinner timings, and how is it possible to leave early to avoid falling asleep (an unexpected telephone summons won't work)?

The telephone trick is pathetic and only effective if you are a good actor, which explains why it is always used in films. Explaining an excuse is always a mistake: remember 'thou doth protest too much'. Much better just to say 'We must leave: thank you so much' and do not even begin to explain, because the absence of an explanation is best interpreted as something personal and sensitive, therefore excusable. If you want to pile it on a bit, you can either contrive a couple of choking coughs or a distinct limp as you rise from your seat. If your host were to be recalcitrant, then awkwardly whisper something like: 'I really am very sorry, but I might have something contagious.' That would be decisive.

The most daring and effective stratagem is what Mark Birley (the London club owner) used to do: he simply got up and made everyone believe he could only be going to the loo, because of his silence, only to discover much later that he had in fact gone home.

It would, however, be rude if you fell asleep at the dinner table. I once nodded off into a snoring slumber in the middle of a tedious conference call for a board meeting and was awoken by the laughter of my fellow directors at the other end of the speaker phone. You don't want to be caught by your fellow diners *in flagrante delicto*.

How do I get rid of my dinner guests when they linger round the dinner table, seemingly not wanting to leave while I am getting more and more tired and wanting to go to sleep?

What I always do is to retire to the bedroom and change into my pyjamas. I then reappear at the table, declaring that I am going to bed and that those who want to go can go, and those who want to stay can stay, with the last person making sure that the front door is closed. This usually has the immediate effect of everyone being embarrassed and getting up to leave. It is so much better to make your guests be the last to feel embarrassed, and not yourself.

• • •

In your column, you had the temerity to call a reader a 'fool' in print. If this is what we can expect from your advisory we are better off without said advice. We may as well get Guns N' Roses to contribute.

I will indeed ask Mr Axl Rose who, when calm, is a most excellent fellow. I once sat my mother-in-law next to him at dinner. She had absolutely no idea who he was.

ETIQUETTE

'What is the proper way to enter a seating row in an orchestra hall when many patrons are already seated?'

IF I WERE TO let out a loud burp towards the end of a repast, I would hope to do so among Chinese or Indians, who wouldn't care, rather than among the English or the French, who would regard it as rude. Same with slurping, especially over noodles: while the practice is acceptable throughout Asia, it's not really good manners to do so in most European countries. In America, I suspect it depends on whether one is eating with obese people or not.

The point I am illustrating is that etiquette is relative, certainly among nations and races. And there have been many misunderstandings arising from ignorance and not doing what the 'Romans do in Rome'. The Prince of Wales once gave me as a present a gold clock from Cartier. It came in a beautiful red leather case. Yet no Chinese would ever offer a clock for a present, and none of us would ever accept a clock as a present, because the phrase 'to give away a clock' is synonymous with 'sending you to death'. So by Chinese tradition, I would effectively be accepting a curse of death. Mind you, I was too oleaginous to refuse the present, although eventually I had to bring the matter to closure by asking the Prince to accept a coin from me as a token of payment for the clock, so that I had, in the eyes of the Chinese God, bought the instrument and not accepted it as a gift. It was an inscrutable way out for keeping the gleaming gold clock.

But etiquette within culture is sometimes regarded by the Establishment as sacrosanct. There is no country more conscious of etiquette than Britain, because her habits and customs and traditions are steeped in history. Debrett's, founded in 1769, has long published *Debrett's Peerage* – regarded as the snooty bible – containing the genealogy of every titled family in the land. In the mid-1900s, it also published a slender volume of advice on entertaining, corresponding, modern manners and more esoteric topics such as being a gentleman, which I remember reading when I was a boy at boarding school. Recently, it has also published a volume on modern manners in order to register the changes that modern life has brought about.

Most of it is sensible, but who on earth would take all the pointers seriously? More to the point, would anyone actually enjoy reading a catalogue of 'dos' and 'don'ts'? Do people still care? Astonishingly, I have found that a great many people do care. And I have discovered it through the piles of missives I have received over the years for my column in the *FT*. Lots of people seem to worry about behaving properly, and they are keen to find out what is regarded as right.

Of course I never know all the answers. I merely try to emphasize that etiquette is ultimately a sensible form that has done no harm to the coexistence of people within the same tribes, for etiquette is definitely tribal. But there are clearly serious rules of etiquette as opposed to frivolous rules of etiquette. So to refrain from murdering someone is obviously a serious rule of etiquette all of us ought to observe, whereas cancelling a dinner party at the last minute is a relatively minor breach of etiquette. My advice is always to use common sense and, when in doubt, choose the most light-hearted or funniest response.

GIFTS

Is it too late to give someone a wedding gift two years after they are married? Or is it better late than never?

First, make sure that the couple is not yet divorced or divorcing. If they are, keep a low profile and you'll be let off the hook.

Otherwise, you must send your present. If you wish to cheat, get something engraved with the date of the wedding, and then pretend with a scream that you had thought all along that the present had been sent to the newly-weds. But if you wish to be smooth, get a top restaurant to connive with you by asking its manager to send the couple a dinner invitation for two, intriguing them with the fact that it is to be hosted *in absentia* by a mystery friend. Then, reveal your identity nonchalantly afterwards. The couple is bound to be impressed by your stylishly late present above all the other timely ones.

The principle 'better late than never' is always a good one, except for the coffin, which is always better never than late.

When you go to a party and bring a wrapped present, is the host supposed to open it in front of you so as to thank you on the spot?

Don't you think that would be far too keen and slightly vulgar? So the answer is no. You don't stand around fishing for compliments but politely leave your present on a side table, nonchalantly, if you know how.

What is the correct etiquette when it comes to 'celebrating the recently departed'? Is wearing black still expected and is this only at funerals but not at memorials? Should one send flowers to the church where they are appreciated for a nanosecond or to the wake where they are really useful/needed?

Wearing black is de rigueur at funerals and memorials, although I have noticed it has also become the standard uniform of shop assistants and waiters in 'trendy' establishments. It is rather disconcerting to feel one is shopping or eating in a funeral parlour which, for me, is always decorated and presented in utter misery.

First, there is the usual irritating organ arrangement of Bach's 'Air on the G String'; followed by 'directors' who, invariably dressed in ill-fitting suits with oleaginous manners, talk in whispers, supposedly to induce an air of decorum and respect. Then there are the ghastly arrangements of flowers, especially of gladioli (because they last long), and the faux-leather Chesterfield or cheap chintzy armchairs with antimacassars. It is high time for funeral directors not to be deadbeat and to modernize their reception rooms. I am thinking minimalistic, with Rothko-like paintings or mini-scale Serra sculptures, all abstract and conceptual, to evoke a reflective mood. The idea is to allow the mourners to meditate in an environment that comforts them into believing their departed kin or friend is floating around in the ether in our Milky Way, in some state of nirvana that we ourselves would not mind getting into. So get rid of all those semi-bijou decorations and go avant-garde; and if unsure, just watch *2001: A Space Odyssey* and copy its rooms in science-fiction mode. Off with the Bach and get some Schoenberg or Berg going, although Strauss's *Also Sprach*, used in the film, should be resisted on grounds of cliché. But Orff's ridiculous *Carmina Burana* could be an inspired choice for pagan mourners, especially those who wouldn't appreciate *Salome* or *Wozzeck*.

And don't send flowers, as they are common, and certainly not on the day. Send whatever else the day before to the bereaved. I often settle for an old volume of poetry, but probably not Sylvia Plath, and I would recommend David Owen's anthology that cleverly follows Shakespeare's seven ages of man. Or to cheer things up, a bunch of old *Mad* magazines, still the funniest with Alfred E. Neuman and Don Martin. Laughter is vital at wakes.

Should one take scatter cushions to a friend who is in prison? Or a throw to jolly up the cell? Do you have experience of such things?

High-security prisons do not allow gifts inside the cell but, for institutions in which scatter cushions, etc., are allowed, the normal interior decor rules must apply: therefore you will need to find out about the colour scheme of your friend/relation's cell and, where applicable, the colour of the inmates' uniforms. Which brings me on to the rule that I have outlined in earlier columns: cushions, scattered or otherwise, should never be placed in the diamond position. They should always be placed square on. Last time I went visiting a very old friend, who was jailed as a dishonest judge, I was prevented from leaving him a book, even though I argued that St Augustine's *Confessions* was a great book for prisoners.

And imagine trying to leave an illegal shahtoosh behind for the likes of Martha Stewart. Would she complain if its colour didn't match her prison garb? Or, God forbid, if the zebra/arrowed/orange/or whatever uniforms clashed with the usually geometric borders of the shahtoosh? And how would any celebrated inmate wrapped in such luxury get up to the bars of the cell window in order to be photographed by the paparazzi? I must now be much more observant in my next visit to a prison and pay attention to its decorative surroundings. I would love to be commissioned by an avant-garde warder to design a set of corridors and cells for a prison. The whole concept of incarcerated functionality would open up a new horizon for interior decor.

Outside the world of prisons, I think of Bayreuth, the Bavarian home of Wagnerism, where cushions are de rigueur because *The Ring* lasts for 30 hours, and all the seats are hard, wooden and without armrests.

TABLE MANNERS

I was told at a dinner one should not fold one's napkin after the meal – it shows that you are not used to having staff who would be cleaning after you. What are your thoughts on table manners?

I come from the middle class, but detest most of its insular philosophy. Who would care about how a napkin is left after a repast? And having staff cannot possibly mean that you have to make work for them. The only thing one must never do with a napkin is to allow it to be folded by a waiter or staff into a triangle and placed by them on to your lap. It's as bad as propping one's cushions up like diamonds.

Regarding table manners, shun such rules as invented by Julian Fellowes on how not to tilt the soup-plate away from you. It's only impractical because it marginally increases the chance of your spilling the soup, and hardly a convention on being polite, whose *raison d'être* is being considerate and not measured by the coefficient of the angular incline of the soup-plate.

As I have become older, I find it difficult to eat soup in the conventional way, ie with a spoon. Do you think it is acceptable to serve soup in a small bowl and sip from it?

As a professor of soup, which I eat every day, I am all for drinking it out of a cup or a mug or a bowl with ears. The only problem is when there are bits such as dumplings in the soup. A large wonton could be testing without a spoon, particularly on those with dentures. But as far as etiquette is concerned, I am always in favour of common sense rather than pointless conventions.

What is the etiquette about having food wrapped and taken away from a restaurant, especially a smart one? Is it acceptable to ask the host, and would it be embarrassing?

Common sense should always rise above conventional niceties. And taking away unfinished food from a restaurant is not only common sense but good sense, given that wastage is wanton in our modern world in which so many go without. In America, portions are obscenely large, which typifies their excesses and explains their rampant obesity: I was once served a T-bone steak whose top bar extended on to the plate of my neighbour! But strangely enough, I notice that in Manhattan many wives, particularly those with plastic surgery, always have their unfinished bits wrapped up for their pets. So only the other day, when a guest of mine at the Savoy Grill whispered to me to ask whether she could have her steak wrapped, I immediately commandeered the waitress, who smartly obliged as a matter of course. But then I turned to my guest and asked what kind of dog she had. She replied: 'Oh no! It's for my own supper!'

If your service in a restaurant includes paper napkins, do you lay one on your lap like you do with cloth ones?

A 'napkin' that is made of paper is not a napkin but a piece of tissue, for which the correct predicate is 'wipe' and not 'lay'. So now you can be clear about what you can do with it.

I have a question about the appropriate use of a fork. While eating, I am in the habit of using my fork like a spoon; placing food in the concave side. My mother has informed me that this is not polite and that I should load food on the back of the fork. I am confident that my mother is correct

about the traditional use of the fork but surely convenience is more important? If a fork is not to be used like a spoon then why is it curved?

I once saw the Queen push three peas up the back of her fork, and therefore I suppose that practice has the royal seal of approval. So you should do as your mother directs if you want to be filial and aristocratic, especially if you want to be a queen!

The practice of eating on the concave side of the fork originated from the American way of eating in which you cut things up and then swap the fork to your right hand, or the dominant hand. I find myself adopting this way of eating because it is rather practical, even if it is American. I must say that if you look at yourself in a mirror while eating off the concave side of the fork, the action looks somewhat odd and inelegant. I don't know why; it just does. But of course looking in the mirror to see how one looks when eating is in itself slightly odd.

As a European living in the US, when dining with Americans I am confronted with them using their knives and forks in a different manner. They cut the same way but then lay down their knife and fork and transfer their fork to the right hand to feed themselves. Should I conform to the custom of my host country or should I keep to the tradition I have maintained my whole life?

Would you eat with your hands in India when everyone else round the table does the same? If you would, then you might do what the Romans do in Rome and follow the American way. If you wouldn't, then just carry on and use your own knife and fork. Who cares? There is too much snobbery about the use of cutlery. It doesn't really matter as long as you don't shove the food into your gob in loud slurping noises. For us Chinese, genteel silence is seldom part of our eating manners. Sometimes even some of my more refined tycoon friends make absolutely disgusting hawking noises or spit out the tiny bones of a duck's web. When I encounter the display of such basic instincts, I often engage a counter-attack by burping out loud. This usually causes a great deal of laughter and jollies up the repast.

What is the standard position to place knife and fork on a plate after finishing a meal or course: should the fork be placed with the points of the tines pointing up or down? Standard procedure seems to indicate 'points up'. But in the spirit of not pointing at anybody with the knife or fork I would prefer tines curving down. What is your advice?

My advice is that there are quite a number of things you ought to worry about before fretting over the position of a fork on a plate, particularly if the plate is empty! I can assure you that the final curvature of the tines would only be detected by a Sherlock Holmes of waiters or butlers. And there ain't too many of them.

Is it acceptable to eat sandwiches in public? Is the answer to turn each rushed lunchtime into a picnic?

Of course it is acceptable to eat a sandwich in public. Maybe not a club sandwich as that would inevitably involve some ugly contortion of the face and probably foods messily falling out of one's mouth. If you go to Japan during the blossoming times in spring, you will see all the Japanese eating outdoors like one gigantic picnic under the prolific blossoms. The ritual is known as Hanami. And Japanese sandwiches are delicious.

I have always admired the sandwich because one can eat it with one hand, just like a hot dog or a pizza. A Chinese takeaway, however, requires two hands to eat: one to hold the container and the other a spoon, fork or pair of chopsticks. Many years ago, I thought about inventing a Chinese takeaway that required only one hand to eat. I attended a course on lateral thinking with Edward de Bono, who famously champions the idea on his island in Venice. The outcome, after three days of deliberations, was a savoury ice-cream cone into which one could put sweet-and-sour pork, chilli beef or chicken with cashew nuts. This would enable one to eat a Chinese takeaway with one hand. But somehow I wasn't entirely convinced by the concept, and never followed it through. Maybe now that I have spilled the beans on the secret, others might do it in my stead. But you heard it here first.

Regarding the reader asking you if it was acceptable to eat sandwiches in public, I strongly disagree with you. An educated person never, ever eats in public or in the street.

Please don't be idiotic. Of course it is perfectly fine to munch a sandwich in the vast openness of the hills, the moors or on a beach. If you go walking in the Lake District, you will definitely need sustenance en route. No educated person would find that disagreeable. In fact, I often like eating a Cornish pasty on a bench at a railway station with the wife. It is very romantic to do so while watching hoi polloi pass by. In fact, it is almost essential when waiting for interminably delayed trains.

MEETING AND GREETING

I suffer from a chronic inability to remember names. What should I do if I am caught cold and have to make an introduction when I have forgotten not one but both names?

I am afraid I am exactly the same. I am thoroughly bad at remembering people's faces and names. Perhaps the least clumsy way of getting over remembering a name is actually to call someone by the first name that comes into your mind. You would say 'Hello, Michael', and the other person would say 'Not Michael: Nicholas!' Then you would immediately say 'I mean Nicholas of course' – as if it were a lapse of the tongue, rather than memory. (Once, the man I called Michael was actually Michael! How clever was that!)

As an agony uncle, you can probably advise on the merits and etiquette of reminding an acquaintance of a brief meeting some 25 years ago.

I have a terrible memory for faces and names, and can never remember who anyone is, unless you were Eva Herzigova. I always get away with the line: 'You Westerners all look alike!' But you won't, if you are not Chinese or oriental. So there is virtually no chance of my being able to remember a brief encounter 25 years ago, let alone remind the person! The only brief encounter I know is between Trevor Howard and Celia Johnson in that gloomy British Rail affair, unconsummated despite the pounding of Rach 2.

What is the etiquette of greeting gamblers in a casino? I have heard of many superstitions and am keen to know how to behave impeccably.

There are indeed a few mortal sins of bad feng shui as far as gamblers are concerned, particularly involving Chinese, who are well known to be the cognoscenti as well as addicts. And you don't want to offend them if they are triads. The first thing you mustn't do is to ask how they are doing! If they are winning, they would regard it as a jinx; if they are losing, they would count it as a continued bad wish. Putting your hand on their shoulders is even worse, as that would signify more burden of bad luck. On a win, it is a mortal offence to exclaim 'well done', as that would be construed as tempting fate and certain to bring about an immediate punishment for arrogance. So best not to speak or shake hands, as you would be naturally and unwittingly saying 'How are you?'

A smile or a nod at a distance is the most sophisticated way of acknowledging the gambler who would be ungrateful for any untoward faux pas. When I was 20 at university, I lost everything I had, including the flat my grandfather bought me. When he sent his lawyer to inspect what I had bought, I had to borrow one from a friend and pretend ownership with the substitution of all the photographs for the visit.

GOING OUT

Is it wrong to leave a play after the first interval on realizing there are two intervals to follow? I am inclined at my age not to be bourgeois, and up sticks and leave early from the theatre, no matter how much I am enjoying myself. No play can possibly last more than two and a half hours – we are not listening to Wagner for goodness' sake. What are your views?

It is dangerous to expose yourself as a total cultural ignoramus, because there are of course plays which can last for more than just the first interval of an hour and a bit. Are you really suggesting that all of Shakespeare's plays should be guillotined? It would be physically impossible even for their words to be uttered within an hour and a bit. And stop throwing names like Wagner around, as if you would stay for any part of his *Ring*, which spans four days and over 25 hours. I don't think you have ever heard Wagner, still less been to Bayreuth. Your pathetic approach to concentration is like saying to all the pilgrims on the Camino de Santiago that they should telescope their month's journey to a day. If I were ever to meet you and find you creeping out of a theatre during the interval, I would call social services to keep you at home.

What is the proper way to enter a seating row in an orchestra hall when many patrons are already seated? Private parts facing those seated or buttocks? (Many do not stand as a courtesy, including women.) I find both somewhat offensive, particularly when I am seated and standing or when sliding aside is often difficult given the tight spacing of the rows. Ahem, with sometimes – too often – offensive odours following. A reason to keep a box, surely, but often not practical.

There is no satisfactory solution, especially when the gap between the rows is tight, which is indeed usually the case in a concert hall or theatre. So you might contrive to get to your seat at the last possible moment yourself and become the late-comer. Then the lesser of two evils is definitely sliding through facing the stage because then at least you wouldn't be caught by an ocean of eyes giving you funny looks. Besides it's easier to arch forward than backwards. The only disadvantage is, as you point out, the possibility of any involuntary fragrant activation on your part. That would be most unfortunate and the only thing to do would be to get to your seat as quickly as possible and look dramatically dismayed in order to create the impression that somebody else is the culprit.

Wearing a box would be a little too dramatic. Just consider its scratching sound against the back of the seats. Your suggestion reminds me of the time when the captain of England's women's cricket team was asked to name the equivalent of the box that she and her team would wear. Her answer: 'a manhole cover'!

I have also been offered solutions for barging into the middle of the row at the theatre. A correspondent suggested the 'easy' solution of booking seats in the middle and arriving at least two hours early. How stupid and ludicrous can this be? It's always difficult enough to get to the theatre on time, let alone arrive two hours early. OK if you were a couch potato, but I ain't one.

Every so often, I meet up with five former colleagues for lunch. Usually, people order dishes that cost roughly the same and the group splits the bill. However, there is one woman who often takes advantage and orders more extravagantly. This happened recently when she ran up a bill more than twice the average. How would you handle such a moocher?

This is a question about 'going Dutch', whose origin comes from the Netherlands where farmhouse doors are always split in half. Hence the assumption of equal proportion. But the rule does not disallow any individual of the group to spend more than the average. Indeed, the rule might even suggest that one would be stupid to be abstemious. So you cannot blame the person who ends up ordering more extravagantly than others, because you could have done so yourself. You must either put up with the final bill and admire the cunning member for getting more than her 'fair' share, or shut up.

Anyone who overspends in a group that is 'going Dutch' is going against the spirit of an evening out shared by friends. It is grossly inconsiderate because some of the party have obviously got less money than others, and it's hard enough

finding a restaurant that suits all pockets and tastes. So I would say that the repeat offender is not being a good friend.

It might have escaped your naivety that it is usually those with less money who order the more expensive items in a group 'going Dutch', as they know it is an opportunity to get better value for money. So are they being inconsiderate by making the richer pay more? Robin Hood would disagree with you.

When I was at university, all of us who went out together were fairly broke. So there was little discrepancy between our means and we never argued about splitting the bill. Once we went to the Italian restaurant Sale e Pepe in Knightsbridge. We knew we couldn't afford its prices but it was a beautiful restaurant with beautiful people, so as young men we wanted to soak ourselves in beauty. When the bill came we were rather surprised by its size because we thought each of us had been abstemious. So we demanded a recount. When the manager returned, the bill was revised upwards – they had left out a couple of drinks and a pudding! We were really irritated for being too clever by half.

I once had Peking duck at a five-star hotel in Macau. When the bill arrived I was surprised to find that I had been charged for having extra pancakes, sauce and sliced cucumber condiments. What are your thoughts on this nickel-and-dime practice?

I think your attitude is a little petty. Just pay for them.

TIPPING

I am new to the sport of shooting and want to get all the ancient traditions right. Can you help? I understand that

there is a peculiar way that you have to tip the gamekeeper at the end of the day. I am very generous, but need guidance on what to give and how to give it with that funny handshake. How should I dress? Do I need my own tweed?

Always look at the gamekeeper straight in the eye, flattering him with either quality or quantity of birds, or both – and at the same time, extending your hand with your banknotes folded up as many times as you can, effecting a suggestion of 'a bundle' of notes. The daily amount should be at least a 'Sir John Houblon' [first governor of the Bank of England – his image appears on the £50 note], with proportionately more if a bag exceeds 400. For dress, wear the oldest ones you have, or else buy something from a second-hand shop. There is nothing more awkward at a shoot than appearing in something spanking new, and bringing urban incongruity to the rural wholesomeness.

What is the tipping etiquette in casinos – at the gaming tables; for complimentary meals?

The law of tipping croupiers has only just come into effect in Britain, so it's a new etiquette to be learned – unlike seedy Macau, whose croupiers curse when you don't tip enough! My recommendation is to tip, as in a restaurant, 5 to 10 per cent, as you get up from the table to cash in – not before, as you should not be obliged to tip if you lose. As for meals, never be greedy. I always gauge my bill, and tip the same amount or even a bit more so that I can have a clear conscience against the casino. I always think it pathetic when people brag that they get 'complimentary' meals, which implies that casinos must be stupid in giving away something for nothing. That, I can assure you, is not a principle by which they operate – and they always get you in the end, whether you pay or not. The psychology is that if you don't pay, you feel that you have had something free, and so you can afford to spend a bit more on gambling. How stupid can you get?

I have never been able to resolve the issue of whether one should tip rude waiting staff and/or poor fare served at a fancy restaurant.

J. S. Mill's principle of utilitarianism dictates that you should always tip irrespective of service, because all of the staff depend on tips to make up their pay. But there are also different practices to be observed. In the US, especially in the Big Apple, extra tips are expected over and above the standard gratuity automatically added to the bill.

Once when I was young, I gave a precocious dinner at Le Cirque in New York when I did not leave any extra tip, because I had assumed the English practice that a standard 10 per cent sufficed. But while saying goodbye to my guests outside the restaurant, a waiter rushed out and interrupted by asking, sarcastically, 'Was there something wrong with our service, sir?' while waving my bill. It was rather embarrassing and I had to rustle up a few greenbacks to pacify the belligerent waiters, and believe you me, there are belligerent waiters in Noo Yawk! The occasion was particularly memorable because Richard Nixon, who was also dining in the restaurant, was adjacent on the pavement, preparing to leave. He seemed to throw me one of his 'expletive deleted' glances against my apparent parsimony before getting into his limo in a shadow of unimpeachable contempt.

CORRESPONDENCE

What is the etiquette of writing thank-you letters in this modern electronic age? Is it acceptable simply to send an

email in lieu of posting a letter, or even just a text or voice message?

My overriding concern regarding thank-you missives is their content, rather than their mode of conveyance. I believe that any writing that induces that stodgy feeling of bread-and-butter is never good enough, nor the kind replete with clichés or filled with superlatives that are no longer superlatives because they have been hacked to death: words such as 'fabulous', 'amazing', 'incredible' or 'unbelievable'. It irritates me no end when I hear the words 'incredible' or 'unbelievable' being used to describe perfectly credible and believable circumstances.

My point is that we must always take some care in crafting our verbal gratitude, otherwise we are doing something merely perfunctory, and not offering genuine thankfulness, which always requires a little effort. Therein lies the real ingredient of good manners, to wit, making an effort to be considerate.

I have a very simple rule about writing any thank-you letter: never use the words 'thank you'. Or at least not until the very end. This simple rule will force the writer to think a bit about what to write. It will also make a difference to the recipient, who must be drowned with letters that begin with the words 'thank you'. On the whole, you will find that avoiding those two hackneyed words will make the letter much more interesting, or at least less pedestrian, because the writer is then diverted to mentioning observations and experiences, thereby flattering the host or hostess into believing that their meticulous preparations have not gone unnoticed. After all, they will most appreciate hearing exactly how their guests have experienced their hospitality. So coming up with the right content is the secret of a fine thank-you missive, rather than just an expression of gratitude.

Invoking a quote, using litotes or including a witticism are all specific ways in which a missive of thanks could become most effective. Indeed, that should be the eternal aim: to make the reader smile when reading what you write.

On the mode of dispatch, I would have thought that for most occasions, it is now acceptable to substitute a letter for an email. Virtually all my friends use emails although I admire those who still hold out. My friend Jools Holland is one. But he does live in a castle. Another is Dame Fanny Waterman. And she is a spring chicken at the age of 95.

I suppose, on very formal occasions, one should still stick to proper writing paper and ink. If I won the Nobel Prize, which I know I shan't, but if I did, I think I might write to the academy and its committee to express my gratitude. But how about the Oscar? To whom does a winner write? George Bernard Shaw was the only man who ever received a Nobel Prize AND an Oscar. Of all people, I would love to know if he wrote to thank anyone.

Finally, if I had just stayed with a prime minister, a monarch or the Pope, a neat letter in ink would be called for.

Would you please elaborate why one should never start a thank-you letter with the words 'thank you'?

Starting a thank-you letter with the words 'thank you' makes you lazy. Also, after you have made your thanks, you have peaked and need to finish. What is much more effective, surely, is to import a crescendo of some sort so that your missive builds up to the climax of the thanks. President Obama was sent Yann Martel's book *Life of Pi*, and in his letter to the author, he wrote: 'Mr Martel, My daughter and I just finished reading *Life of Pi* together. Both of us agreed we prefer the story with animals. It is a lovely book – an elegant proof of God, and the powers of storytelling. Thank you. Barack Obama.'

See how the 'thank you' goes at the end and not at the beginning!

Indeed, if you search online for 'famous letters of thanks', you will find that 90 per cent of them do not start with the words 'thank you', and the best ones never do.

A titled friend has remarried after a divorce. Of course it is first names all round whenever we meet, which is easy. However, when it comes to writing out formal invitations should her new ladyship be so addressed? And still the same with regard to his first wife?

Simple. The new wife takes the title of your titled friend. And the divorced wife is entitled to use her old titled name until she remarries. So it is possible for there to be two Lady Xs at the same time. What is not correct is the common use, and very common it is too, of the first name and the surname together when one is not the daughter of an earl or upwards. Ergo, the wife of Sir Philip Green is properly Lady Green, but definitely not Lady Tina Green.

I have a social dilemma. I wish to address a letter to Tang Wing, otherwise known as Sir David Tang. As he is a Sir, this introduces a dilemma in that I ordinarily start my letters to male persons as 'Dear Sir'. Would this show the right degree of deference or do you address a Sir as 'Dear Sir Sir' in letters?

First, my Chinese name is Tang Wing-Cheung (meaning 'forever brilliant'!). My grandfather, who was also knighted, was known in Hong Kong as Sir Tang, which of course was inconsistent with the established British practice of using the given name after the title. So he should have been Sir Shui-Kin.

Anyway, if you were writing to someone you didn't know, you would indeed address them as 'Dear Sir'. If you knew you were writing to me, you could address your opening as 'Dear Sir David'. Or even 'Dear Sir David Tang', which is less obsequious. And if you knew me, 'Dear David' would be perfectly acceptable. As for all my friends, they of course just write 'Dear Tang' or something much more derogatory like 'Dear Fatso'. I have always wished I had another son, whom I would have named Price – so that if he were to be knighted, he would become 'Sir Price' Tang!

How many Christmas cards did you receive? Do you send out as many? What do you do with them afterwards?

My wife and I long ago became too lazy to send Christmas cards, in the hope of receiving fewer. But it hasn't happened. We get loads. I immediately jettison those sent with catalogues or in blatant disguise as trade, and those with no signature or with a printed signature. On the whole, it is simply not worth keeping any card without one's name inside. Otherwise, I keep all the funny ones and mostly the ones with photographs of ugly children or ageing parents or, thankfully, dogs. Yes, we only really love the ones with dogs. But at Epiphany, the whole lot is tipped into the wastepaper basket.

MANNERS

What is the best response to unsolicited phone calls from those trying to sell you something? Is there a standard way to deal with bad telephone manners?

When I get someone trying to peddle some dubious product on the telephone, I routinely leave it off the hook and just ignore the babbling, which will come to a natural end when the peddler realizes that he or she is talking to the ether. Also irritating is when someone rings you and asks: 'Who's that speaking?' My standard reply is: 'You are.'

Few things annoy me more than lateness, particularly when the person being late doesn't even twig that they may have caused inconvenience, offence or my blood to boil. What are your thoughts on lateness? Do I need to just get over it?

You would be silly not to notice that there are two groups of people in the world – those who are always punctual, and those who are always late. For those who keep their time, they always have a genuine excuse and apologize for being late. But for those who are always late, you should never get into a stew. I'd say: 'If you cannot beat them, then beat them just as they think you are going to join them.' Therefore, you should be later still. Just gauge how much they are always late by, and aim to arrive 10 to 15 minutes afterwards. And you don't apologize. If they should even begin to complain, you can chuck the entire book of hypocrisy at them.

How should a gentleman respond to finding out that he has been the victim of a cruel practical joke?

A real gent would take a practical joke in his stride, although occasionally it might not be ungentlemanly to resort to revenge. That's what Steed, the Avenger carrying his signature bowler and brolly in a Savile Row suit, always did. We must not, however, be too hasty in exacting revenge, which is best served cold. A very good friend of mine, whose wife introduced me to my wife, worked for the Prince of Wales, and on a few occasions he would telephone me imitating the voice of the heir to the throne – with devastating accuracy. Every time he did it, I was too gullible and unctuous to disbelieve that the Prince would telephone me. I would politely carry on the conversation, gesticulating to anyone else in the room to keep quiet. Then suddenly there would be booming laughter at the other end of the line with my friend obviously curled up in a foetal position for succeeding with his impression. I fell for the joke a couple of times and was determined not to be caught out again. The day after the death of my father, I received a phone call which I was convinced was another of my friend's vocal pranks. So I let him carry on sending me his condolences, then I bellowed down the line: 'Sure sure, Guy, and you know where you can shove your condolences?' – before slamming down the phone. It turned out that, on this singular occasion, it was actually the Prince who had called.

My wife and I recently attended a performance of Handel's *Messiah* at St Thomas Church on Fifth Avenue, New York. Sitting in front of us was a couple that whispered occasionally during the performance but at one point began what was almost a conversation. I tapped the woman on the shoulder, received no acknowledgement and was about to do so again when my wife grabbed my arm and, bowing to a cooler head, I desisted. The nattering ceased and I began to enjoy the superb performance. I was later told that I shouldn't have touched the offending party. Could you please advise on the correct procedure/protocol in dealing with a similar situation, given that I did not wish to make a noise and was lacking pencil and paper?

Tapping involves contact and is technically the beginning of an assault. Better to lean forward and just make the 'Shhh' noise.

You can first do so pianissimo then, if the disturbance persists, follow it with a longer fortissimo. If it still doesn't work then bring out your extended selfie stick and protrude it in front of the offenders, behind whom you might contort your face and stick your tongue out. Then post and expose them on social media as noise pariahs.

I also encounter insufferable noises and smells in cinemas: packets of crisps, boxes of chocolate and, worst of all, stinking hot dogs or tortilla crisps with salsa! They totally ruin one's peace and quiet in the darkness for an hour or two. I now sometimes bring a torch and strobe it around the culprits.

But going back to oratorios, did you know that in Bach's days, when *St Matthew Passion* was performed, the entire audience or congregation was expected to stand up and join in the famous chorus. I did that last at St John's Smith Square in London, and it really was exciting to have a few hundred people rising to sing the chorus – three times in all.

I am a fan of US college football and often find myself sitting behind uncouth, inconsiderate people who stand up when nobody else is, thereby blocking the views of everyone behind. How do I get these boors to comply with my polite requests to sit? They often respond with a rude comment, at which point I mercilessly harass them until they comply. I would like to know an easier way. With football season on the way, your answer could make my weekends much more pleasant.

I don't know about American football spectators, but if you were at a football match in England, I would think twice about being assertive. It could be argued that England invented the football hooligan, and, given their reputation, English hooligans might as well be the direct descendants of the Vikings. So unless one feels like being Genghis Khan, one should sit tight and suffer these human eclipses. You are already doing well in the US to dare show anger and demonstrate harassment. So keep it up! There is no easier way.

I'm in somewhat of a quandary over neighbours who live in an apartment beneath my penthouse. Since my wife and I moved in, we have invited them up for drinks on three occasions. Each time we commenced the evening with champagne, moving on to fine Bordeaux and finally a stiff brandy for the road (or swaying staircase in their case). Genial and travelled they may be, yet offering return invites to their place has never happened. One doesn't like to impose, or God forbid suggest, that it's their turn. Do we say something outrageous, perhaps suggesting a popular relative passed away and we're holding on to him? And that, what with the smell and the heat, theirs might be better next time?

How stupid of you to keep inviting them! You must have some ulterior motive, conscious or subconscious. Could it be that you are attracted to the wife? Or your wife to the other husband? Do I detect an undercurrent of a potential affair or even wife-swapping, which I gather is not uncommon in the depths of suburbia? Might you be writing from Surbiton? Could there be a *crime passionnel*? If so, instead of your joke, you might end up with a dead wife and a stench. The only advice I give is that if this is what you intend to do, execute it in France where *crime passionnel* is apparently a legal defence.

My wife and I (both in our early 70s) recently spent a weekend in London. One morning we had breakfast in a

branch of a well-known café chain. The waiter, who was initially very polite, served our order saying: 'Your coffee, sir, and the tea for your mother.' I was speechless. Did I (being Dutch) not grasp the English humour or was this meant to be a compliment to me?

I doubt the waiter was trying to be funny or complimentary to you. It was clearly a faux pas made by a waiter who was half-blind or just plain stupid. The same thing once happened to my wife and me in a hotel. She is 14 years younger than me, and I was mistaken as her father. Given the fact that I am Chinese and my wife English, the manager must have been even more blind or more stupid than your waiter.

What could you do to someone (and it has happened twice in the last week) who, at a small friendly party, produces a cigar and starts to explain to everybody how good, special and expensive it is, and starts smoking it without offering another one to anyone?

The only way to deal with selfish show-offs is to expose their vulgarity. There are two approaches: the elegant way, and the blunt way. For elegance, you might turn to one of your friendly group and make it fairly clear that you are referring to the braggart by quoting a bit of Shakespeare when everyone is listening: 'I do not much dislike the matter, but the manner of his speech.' This of course comes from *Antony and Cleopatra*, and a description of Enobarbus, who was extremely blunt with his soldiers. If, however, your company is rather uneducated, you might choose the blunt approach, in which case, you might bark out something like: 'If your cigar is so good, why don't you stop talking and give us one each, and we will tell you if it is any good.'

I have come to notice that occasionally people with dentures move them on and off in their mouth, which is most disconcerting. What do you do with somebody when they are doing this at a reception? Do you ignore it, or do you say something – and if so, what?

On the assumption that those with dentures are reasonably old, I would tend to exercise the Confucian principle of respect for elders, in which case I would simply ignore it and keep silent. But I must confess that it is a most unsavoury sight to behold, and I suppose one could try a remark such as 'Are your dentures on an elastic band?', ie using humour to mask disdain.

But dentures could become useful in an emergency: the 19th-century palaeontologist Edward Drinker Cope was collecting fossils not far from Little Bighorn, where General Custer met his last stand, when he was confronted by a group of Indians, who obviously harboured a sense of hostility against the white man, until Cope took his dentures out of his mouth and then put them back in, repeating the process like a clown. This did the trick of amusing the forebears of Tonto sufficiently for them to let the collector go without harm.

My personal trainer has a highly ornate tattoo portraying Dante's *Inferno*. I can clearly see the first and second circles on her shoulder, the latter vividly portrayed in a violent storm. I can also see the ninth circle on the bottom of her vest with the traitors frozen in the lake of Cocytus. I am particularly interested to see how the tattooist has approached gluttony and greed. Would it be polite to show an interest and ask to see, or might this offend her?

If your trainer wanted to show off her Dante tattoos, she would have worn an exercise bra and not leave you guessing on most of her circles of hell. The fact that she wears a T-shirt must either be intended to make you curious, or there is something she wants to hide. But I note she chose hell and not paradise or purgatory. This probably means she is temperamentally aggressive or violent, and you must be cautious about any suggestion to lift her veil. If you are fat, you could be self-deprecating by asking about gluttony. Maybe she would be amused enough to let you see how her tattoo treats this sin. But if you are keen to impress her with your literary erudition, you might ask if she ever considered a tattoo of the famous epigraph to 'The Love Song of J. Alfred Prufrock'. You will then have shown off your grasp not only of medieval Italian poetry but also the modern English movement through the seminal T. S. Eliot.

What is the form when one receives, as I did yesterday, a derogatory email about oneself forwarded to one's inbox in error?

Let X be the offender who wrote derogatorily about you, and Y be a well-known reporter of a tabloid newspaper. Send the following email to X, ostensibly in error, and from an anonymous email address: 'Dear Y, I believe I have a story about X which you would be interested in. Please let me know how I can contact you to speak on the phone or meet. I have hesitated about volunteering this information. But after much consideration, I believe that this story on X is in the public interest, and that your readers would like to know. [Signed anonymous.]' And for maximum revenge, send this missive on a Friday afternoon, so that X is rattled all weekend.

· · ·

Is your column morphing into your own soapbox? I can't work out if you are an agony aunt on the niceties of social niceties or platforming your political views. I am confused.

An avuncular oracle on life is what I aspire to, although I know I am still light years away from Delphi. All of our social behaviour is surely influenced by history and politics, and our opinions are never one-dimensionally formed. I also believe we should be relentless in our search for knowledge, and the wider the spectrum we have of life, the better equipped we would be in trying to make a difference. Very grandiose, you might argue, but my conviction is there is no point in mediocrity but every point in meritocracy.

For example, my decorative style has developed through both the occidental and oriental perspectives, and much in the context of their histories, which interweave and influence each other.

The Chinoiserie movement was an obvious product, although it is amusing to discover that it originated from a minor Dutch diplomat who happened to be an excellent sketcher.

Ergo, stop trying to put me in a pigeon hole and desist from lapsing into that ugly American habit of turning a perfectly good noun like 'platform' into a verb.

HOME DECOR/
INTERIORS

*'Is it still acceptable to decorate one's home
with stuffed animals?'*

PERHAPS THE MAIN division among decorators consists of the 'minimalists' and the 'maximalists', whereby the former wish to sprinkle just a few pieces of furniture in a big space, while the latter can't wait to fill the space with fixtures, fittings and objects. I had a head-on collision along these lines with a colleague of mine at the *FT*, Lucy Kellaway, who is an ardent follower of that amazing Japanese decluttering guru, Marie Kondo. Lucy and I visited each other's house and essentially slagged one another off on how we make use of our spaces at home. My conclusion was that I was vehemently against her anxiety to get rid of things, while she could not understand how I could be perfectly comfortable being bombarded by stuff. But I am happy to say that we settled the dispute amicably, agreeing to accept our differences as evidence of the fact that aesthetically there is a whole spectrum of good taste.

And that, I would say, is the first thing to remember when it comes to interior decorations: there are no hard and fast rules. Just as Wittgenstein taught us that it is impossible to say exactly what a game is, but that we would all nonetheless recognize one if we saw one, so too with stylishness, elegance, beauty or charm. There are no necessary or sufficient conditions for any of these concepts, and as such they are not completely definable. My own parallel, incidentally, is the day on which I need to buy a birthday present for my grandmother. I can never think of anything in particular that she would want. But if I went to a department store, especially Tokyu Hands in Tokyo, I am almost certain to come across something that I could point to and say: 'That's what she wants.' Accordingly, I can always tell you what

I feel about an interior once I have seen it, but I wouldn't be able to tell you beforehand exactly what you need.

Ergo, I can't define good taste, just as I can't define a game. But when I see good taste, I am able to say that it is good taste, just as I can point at a chessboard and pieces and say that it is a game. Equally, I am certain I can point out 'bad taste' when I see it. And I see an inordinate amount of it. Bad taste mostly comes from those who do not possess an innate perception for visual satisfaction, or are simply indolent.

When money is no object, fancy designers often succumb to the temptation to concoct an aesthetic disaster and so become the culprits of bad taste. Because they are on percentage commissions on the total amount spent, they often go out of their way to buy the most expensive pieces, without necessarily thinking if they will blend in with the rest of the surroundings. It is not surprising, therefore, to find plenty of gold leaf and metallic walls waging aesthetic war with convoluted chandeliers, or abortive-looking sofas and chairs piled high with a mountain of Versace-esque cushions. The bespoke nature of these monstrosities drives the budgets up, and therefore the designers earn fatter fees. They get away with it due to the insecurity of their mega-rich clients, who think that blowing vast amounts of money on something custom-made constitutes real chic, when half the time it's nothing but ostentatious rubbish.

At the other end of the scale, diminished budgets can force the designer to think more inventively about creating a pleasing aesthetic. Just think of those charming bed-and-breakfasts and continental *pensioni* in which the rooms are simply furnished with decent furniture, the chairs and curtains are in unpretentious fabrics, there are fresh linens and towels in the bathrooms, and pretty original paintings in old frames on the walls. I, for one, would not hesitate for a second to embrace these signs of comfort over ostentation for its own sake. At the end of the day, all that one should be doing in decorating a house is trying to make it as comfortable as possible: 'comfort, comfort, comfort' is just as important as 'location, location, location'.

DECORATION

I would like to ask you two questions, if I may. First, what is your idea of a well-decorated house? Second, which is your favourite philosophy, art of living, or book?

Why don't you ask me a more general question? I don't think this is general enough. Surely, I must be given more latitude.

Yellow and pink do go together, don't they? My daughter is about to put a pink sofa in a Chinese yellow room.

I hope your daughter is an admirer, like me, of Cy Twombly, whose *Untitled (Sunset)*, which he painted in 1986, is a masterpiece of yellow and pink. She will find the same bold collision of these colours in Turner and Monet if she looks closely at their paintings, which exude both spontaneity and exuberance. I certainly prefer rooms with lots of colour, particularly those with the clashing tonalities of a single colour, which is never taught at art schools or on interior design courses, and requires confidence to execute. I love taking several timbres of red, say, and then mixing and matching them together: burgundy, vermilion, scarlet, blood, crimson, sangria, ruby. This certainly beats the dishwater dullness of white-grey-black, which seems to be the yawning standard pattern in show flats, especially those offered to the uber *nouveaux riches*, whose eyes invariably need examining.

I have been approached by a periodical with a request to feature my home and its interiors. Have you ever been tempted to allow such an intrusion? One hears of horror stories when the photographer rearranges your furniture into what they deem to be more appropriate an aspect. Despite the flattery implicit in the request, is it not a little naff?

It is not naff if your home is worth being photographed. The naffness comes from homeowners who have ghastly interiors but believe they are beautiful, and feel the need to impose their bad taste on us, the readers. So, the real answer depends on whether your home is interesting enough. I have often been asked to launder my interiors in magazines although I nearly always say 'no', mainly because they are an intrusion. But if you relent, like I have a couple of times, there are rules on which you must insist.

First, photographers and any 'artistic directors' must not be allowed to start rearranging your furniture or adding to your natural surroundings. Therefore, stop the use of 'props' like a breakfast tray with a glass of orange juice and a rose stem in a tulip glass, resembling a room service trolley, or a throw draped nonchalantly, but awkwardly, across the sofa or bed. These are interfering practices which promote phoniness. Above all, you should not let yourself be dolled up in varying outfits, as one is used to seeing in the pages of popular downmarket weeklies that are better consigned to loos or very dull dentist waiting rooms.

I love my pictures of myself and my family with famous people, but is displaying them on the piano egocentric?

The rule about pictures with famous people is simple: if you are really good friends with them, no problem. But it is infra dig if they were taken at a reception or from an accidental meeting in the street or restaurant or behind a cordon alongside a red carpet! *De minimis*, it has to be in your house, or theirs, or on holiday. But I would make one exception: any photograph with Kim Jong-il, the leader of North Korea, should be enlarged and framed, for he is a very smooth freak to be standing next to, and we would all know that he doesn't know you.

Please settle a debate as the fate of my walls hangs in the balance. I believe that family photographs should never be displayed on walls, but rather on tables. I think photographs look horrid when hung. My husband feels differently. Please apprise as to who is correct.

Old Etonians love hanging pictures of their Houses or sporting teams in their guest loos. Sometimes they also hang family photographs in silly poses or pictures taken at grand occasions. But they are all confined to the lavatories, presumably to exhibit a sort of inverted snobbery. Otherwise, you wouldn't see, at least with anyone U, any family photographs other than in frames designed to rest on surfaces. By far the most offensive types of hanging family photos are those done by so-called 'portrait' photographers who develop their prints on canvases in order to create the impression of an oil painting.

Are the Romanov-style photographs of my friends surrounded by their grandchildren, placed prominently in serried ranks on a grand piano, rather nauseating in this day and age? Please tell me it is unutterably wrong to have photographs on a piano.

It is not wrong to have photographs on a piano, except if one is a concert pianist and wants to open the lid – especially on a Stein-way D, which is 9ft long and probably the most powerful instrument on earth – as it would be very tiresome to have to remove photographs each time. I just put two large frames on mine for ease of removal in case I want to imagine myself being a concert pianist with the majestic lid fully opened as in the Albert Hall. As for the content, I would advise against the Romanov style as all of them were murdered in the wood, and it would be extremely bad feng shui to imitate that grouping.

What's your view of installation art in a private home? I was recently at a function where a server accidentally kicked an acrylic glass skeleton that was displayed on the floor, spilling its bright red 'blood' all over.

I think indoor installations are best consigned to corners, pseuds' corners that is, because they usually involve a great deal of conceptual philosophizing that would bore an insomniac to slumber. At this year's Venice Biennale, I queued up outside the Korean pavilion for half an hour to get into the 'dark room' because there were warnings against epilepsy, faintheartedness, claustrophobia, and these alerts naturally attracted mugs like me. But this 'dark room' consisted of absolutely nothing at all and when we were inside, we did nothing, we heard nothing, we said nothing, and after a few minutes we were all ushered out, with nothing. Codswallop was how I felt, until I realized that such a dark room at my home could be very useful. All of my boring visitors, especially my wife's, could enter it and stay inside until they left. So perhaps artistic fraud could have a practical application.

But I generally like outdoor installations, especially when they are beautiful large pieces in a stunning landscape. Chatsworth occasionally has previews of lots intended for auction and they bring out some of the best spiritual interaction between man and nature, although I wish there were more installations that made us laugh.

You once quoted from Shakespeare's *Antony and Cleopatra*, so it is not entirely a surprise that you have a bust of the Roman general Mark Antony in your home. Do you see it as a reminder of the fact that we are all human mortals, a symbol of a plebeian who ascended to power, an obscure political statement, or do you believe history creates some depth to an interior?

Mark Antony sits on a pedestal in my home because I always hope that anyone there, particularly my wife, will lend me their ears. He also reminds me of Cleopatra whose image, beautified by Elizabeth Taylor in Hollywood, is not one to shun. Cleopatra also reminds me of the most voluptuous painting of all time by Guido Cagnacci, in which he depicts her death in nakedness. And how about that other wonderful painting by Lawrence Alma-Tadema of both Antony and Cleopatra? It is full of mystery and darkness, beauty and provocation.

The point is that features in a room should provoke our imagination so that we can fill our surroundings with shifting images and streams of consciousness. Therefore, I am in full agreement that an air of history does create depth to an interior. Great thinkers are always swimming in artefacts in their pools of writing. That is why the best rooms are always those replete with paintings and books, with content to fill a universe of memories and dreams. Little wonder that it is a cinch to spot those soulless rooms, with abortive lighting and new pieces of furniture that are unmissable in uber-expensive show homes, which are black holes of taste and imagination.

I recently made a remark about a rather terrifying bear head hanging in a friend's country home, to which he replied jokingly: 'It smiles when my wife listens to me.' What are

your thoughts on taxidermy? Is it still acceptable to decorate one's home with stuffed animals?

I hope your friend lives in a huge pile with a baronial hall, for otherwise a stuffed bear head will look out of place and pretentious, however humorous he tries to be. On taxidermy as decoration, I would only recommend it for works of art. It would be splendid if Damien Hirst's life-size stuffed cow floating in formaldehyde were to be found in, say, a massive larder. Or Cai Guo-Qiang's absolutely extraordinary leaping wolves and tigers cascading across a grand entrance hall? But these dream arte-facts are for museums or billionaires.

My modest attempt to introduce taxidermy at home is designed to evoke poetry and consists of a magnificent tiger head, with fiercely translucent eyes and menacing teeth, that almost shouts out William Blake's thumping words: 'Tyger, tyger, burning bright/In the forests of the night/What immor-tal hand or eye/Could frame thy fearful symmetry?' I just love the idea of imagining a God who could create such a beautiful yet fierce animal. So it all counts as art.

What I don't particularly like is seeing those colonial macho hunters who adorn their homes with their conquests, which are redolent of brutality rather than masculinity and steeped in white mischief.

But my biggest problem with stuffed animals is they are frightening in the dark. I don't exactly like to be scared out of my wits. My wife is enough.

FINISHING TOUCHES

What do you think of curtains that are particularly ornate with folds and pleats as extra decorative bits on the pelmets? Should curtains be touching the floor or dragging?

Unless you have a proper country pile, you should never have ornate curtains – and certainly not elaborate pelmets, unless you have a very high ceiling. Particularly laughable are the ones made to look grand in a mock-Tudor mansion at, say, Weybridge, or The Bishops Avenue off Hampstead Heath. Curtains are properly hung when they are half a centimetre above the floor. The crunched-up versions are either appalling ostentations drummed up by pretentious designers or, more acceptably, adapted to fit another space by impecunious aristos.

Is it a bit old-fashioned now to use net curtains? But how do you stop people looking in?

There is something about net curtains that is quintessentially suburban. Whenever I see them, I always expect some nosy parker to be peeping through surreptitiously from behind, looking out. So generally, I am much more concerned with the people inside looking out – rather than those from the outside looking in. This is particularly important in Singapore where, apparently, there is a law forbidding one to change in a light room without curtains, lest it encourages voyeurism. At my homes, I have usually settled for venetian blinds, which are extremely practical as slats can be turned slightly up or down, making it possible for us to see out from the inside, but not nearly as well from the outside looking in. From a decoration point of view, it is always much better to have some form of separation between the house inside and the view outside. It is a classical howler, committed by so many modern designers, especially for hotels with vistas, to install a virgin picture window in front of a marvellous view. This is because only with a separation would one actually appreciate that one was inside – and, paradoxically, have the view enhanced by being interrupted by some kind of lattice. Hence the French window, a wonderful invention that provides precisely the lattice of separation that, against our instinct, enhances rather than impedes the view.

What's your take on door handles versus door knobs?

I have one general rule: bathrooms and lavatories should always have handles because if your hands are wet, it is easier to turn a handle rather than twist a knob, especially with those knobs that are tight to turn. I was once stuck in a lavatory for not being able to twist a knob sufficiently for the door to open, and eventually had to use my mobile phone to call a waiter in the restaurant to open it for me. On this occasion, the door turned out to be a sliding one. I felt rather stupid. Talking of doors, I have always been amused by the title of Quintin Hogg's autobiography, *The Door Wherein I Went*. It sounds like an alternative title to Alfred Hitchcock's film *Psycho*, in which Norman Bates goes around wearing his mother's clothes and a wig and carrying a large kitchen knife. I doubt, however, that Lord Hailsham would have been amused by this parallel – not that I imagine he would have watched *Psycho*. But he would have known all about murder, as it was he who defined it in the statute book. Lord Chancellors, unlike today, used to know a thing or two about the law.

How important is lighting in a home? Are there any useful rules to follow, especially from professional designers who install lighting in restaurants, stores and hotels?

These so-called 'professional designers' always commit the glaring mistake of lighting a room from the ceiling down. Are they blind in noticing that it is highly annoying to see the source of light, which irritates our eyes, and that illumination downwards invariably casts shadows on faces which is never flattering? These problems are further aggravated by the gradual disappearance of warm, standard yellowish light and its substitution with LEDs that resemble more the harsh whiteness of a fluorescent tube. Talking of which, I can offer an explanation as to why Marks and Spencer seems to struggle with its clothing range, despite adverts involving some of Britain's most recognizable icons. The reason, as I once told the chief executive, who obviously did not think much of my logic, is that in every branch of M&S, the prevalent lighting is harsh white light. While this might be acceptable for buying frozen fish fingers, refrigerated chicken korma or even underwear, it is very unflattering for clothing. M&S must introduce soft yellow lighting for these departments. Just look at all the other clothing stores, none of which use white light.

Are cushions with messages acceptable?

Yes, if the messages are embroidered and the words are witty. I have always liked 'If there is a will, there is a relative'. But the best kinds of cushions are those made into small pillows. In my advancing age, I only recently discovered how comfortable they are to sleep with. They are now indispensable, and on these pillows I wouldn't mind embroidery, like Yeats's cloths of heaven, a bit more along the lines of treading softly on one's dreams, or Neruda on writing the saddest lines in the night, or Li Bai on sleeping beneath a beautiful moon. These lines are always best reminded, gently, on the threshold of the Land of Nod. They also provide something intelligent to talk about with one's wife or lover in bed.

I have Einstein's formula $E=mc^2$ sewn in four colours on one of my small pillows. On many occasions, I have tried to explain its significance to my wife. Although she started off with a vague sense of curiosity, she is now bored to tears by still not comprehending either Einstein's genius or my pathetic explanation of his formula. But that is precisely one's cunning way of securing peace and quiet in the spousal bed.

I am rather keen on the burning of incense sticks in a style reminiscent of my navel-gazing youth – floor cushions, kaftans, Moroccan rugs, Leonard Cohen melancholia and Marie Rose sauce – the best are Namche Bazaar by Astier de Villatte. Do you burn, or is it passé?

I love a pervading scent in a room. A raging log fire emits the best natural smell – homely, comforting and snug. But I also love incense, whose resin form I used to buy in the markets of Marrakech, Fez and Tangier. The only problem is that they are quite overpowering, and might have been even in the languishing 1960s of hairy psychedelia to which you allude. So nowadays I cheat with incense sprays and oils that are dropped on to terracotta rings that cleverly fit into the girth of a light bulb.

My taste for incense has come from my early days when I was a regular altar boy swinging the thurible at Mass and Benediction. At the same time, I discovered that incense sticks were also burnt on our Buddhist altar at home where my father, grandmother and great-grandmother prayed. Therefore, I was brought up soaked in incense and cannot get enough of it. So for my scent, I choose Comme des Garçons, which produces five shades of incense all of which I mix up to form a landscape of odours, foxing even the fashion cognoscenti.

Would you agree that silver tea strainers are impractical? The metal is so highly conductive that after filling your cup, the strainer becomes too hot to remove by hand. In

China – the home of tea – nobody seems to care about tea leaves floating around in their cuppa. Perhaps the front rows of teeth act as a natural filter.

That's why one should always let a pot brew for a few minutes to allow the leaves to settle at the bottom before pouring. But if one is a fusspot about the tiniest leaf crumbs getting into the cup, or has no patience for brewing, then try using a silver-coated or even a stainless-steel strainer, which conducts much less than one made of solid silver.

You are right about my compatriots taking tea with no strainer. We don't mind floating leaves. We simply shoo them gently away with whispering eddies. Leaves are always superior when they are whole and do not consist merely of dust, as used in tea bags, which are a camouflage for inferior brews. If one had a spittoon, as did both Chairman Mao and Deng Xiaoping, one could chew up the leaves and spit them into the receptacle. I do admit, however, that if such an action were accompanied by loud hawking from the throat, it wouldn't be exactly elegant. Worse still, as has happened, if a senior cadre's set of dentures were to be ejected inadvertently.

Are garden gnomes acceptable? If so, why so? If not, why not?

I like garden gnomes because they are usually smoking. I also like them because they are the underdogs to gentry snobs, some of whom, without any sense of humour, have seen to it that gnomes are officially banned from the Chelsea Flower Show. I must try to smuggle one in next year. Apparently there are millions of them in Germany from where they originated. Even Wagner must have had them in his subconscious when he created Alberich, a dwarf chief, as the guardian to the treasure of the Nibelungen in *The Ring*. My mother-in-law, who is herself only 4ft 10in, has a couple of non-smoking gnomes on her immaculately manicured lawn in Essex, believing that they would annoy me. But they don't. On the contrary, I am very sympathetic to her seeing her gnomes eye-to-eye.

Scented candles – is it burning money and is it EVER acceptable to scent one's rooms?

Stop worrying about money, which is meant for burning, like desires. A pervading aroma in a room is very welcoming and calming and comfortable. But the only scents I like are natural ones like incense or sandalwood, and I hate the sweet artificial mixture that saturates the candle market. I remember Diana, Princess of Wales, burning scented, tuberose candles at her home at Kensington Palace even at lunchtime. It was one of the chicest things she did.

LUXURY LIVING

Do you ever watch the television programme *Grand Designs*? Do you think it is admirable or reckless that people should take into their own hands the design and building of a 'dream house'?

I used to think they were admirable because they had the guts to take, in effect, DIY to its ultimate level. But having seen many results, I now think they might be reckless after all.

The real problem with any 'grand design' is that it should be regarded as 'grand'. Grandeur is usually a folly unless one is King Louis XIV or King Ludwig II. In the hands of the amateur, scale is particularly difficult to get right. Most of all, when there are conceptual problems in reality, the grand designer tends to soldier on doggedly and conflate determination with stupidity. The worst is when the completed structure requires rectification. Being non-professional in most cases, the grand designer has the propensity to get things wrong. Yet when there are mistakes, there is usually not enough budget or energy left for correction, with the result that the mistakes remain as constant irritants. If only people would return to basics and build symmetrical buildings, or, even better, a courtyard house whose configuration for living together has never been improved. Then they would minimize their chances of getting things wrong.

I also notice that the interior decor in most of these egotistical creations is often pedestrian at best and, at worst, extremely suspect. Such poor results suggest to me that these 'grand designs' are insipid.

There are, however, exceptions of course. The Flint House that Lord Rothschild commissioned at his country estate of Waddesdon, in Buckinghamshire, looks extremely stylish, especially against the surrounding landscape. The interiors are the work of the brilliant David Mlinaric. This is what any 'grand design' should aspire to, although I suspect that the usual conditions of moolah and acreage were not a mortal concern in this case.

My personal preference for a dream house is to look for one, rather than build one myself. The point is that sometimes it is difficult, or even impossible, to define and draw up what a dream house is, although when we see one, we are able to say 'eureka' and point at it with a great sense of discovery. This is similar to the philosophical point made by Wittgenstein, who said that we might not be able to define what a game is, but when we see one, we are able to identify it as a game. Ergo, I cannot tell you exactly what a perfect woman is, but when I see my wife, I am able to point to her and say: 'That's her!'

What do you think about the trend for houses with a gym in them? And what do you think of their decorations? How do they compare with commercial gyms, especially the expensive ones requiring membership that have sprung up in London and other capitals?

I have indeed noticed that a gym is now almost de rigueur in large houses. But what is extraordinary is that they are invariably built in the smallest room of the house, and in the basement with no window – just a giant television screen in front of an unappetizing-looking treadmill with which Sisyphus might have been content. This is a complete misunderstanding of what a gym ought to be. If I had a mansion in London, I would have a gym with a wonderful view, preferably with French windows that could be opened on to a terrace or a garden.

The best exercises are done outdoors, not in a subterranean space with white lighting and mirrors all round, which are now standard decorations. Commercial gyms are worse because they all look identical, with rows and rows of machines set out to resemble a military installation, filled with people who either have strata of fat or egotistical muscles, which are even more unsightly.

I also think it a bad idea to watch television on any exercise machine, because the whole point of exercise is to clear one's mind by allowing time to think without distractions. But then there are the few of us who are fortunate enough to be a member of Mark Birley's 'gym', whose secrets are, thankfully, intact. That's why I can't tell you how things ought to be done, not even in this column.

What are your views about private cinemas at home? Do those people who are in possession of such a luxury feel the need to go to the cinema? Do you have a private cinema at home?

I do not have a private cinema at home. I also think that those of my friends who do continue to go to the cinema have a far superior experience. There are reasons why the private cinema at home cannot be a real substitution. Even though private cinemas are invariably designed with a dozen Pullman seats (which have a disadvantage of making one fall asleep far too easily), a lot of rich people make the mistake of failing to insist on a high ceiling and a lot of black space, as in normal cinemas.

So for me, a private cinema at home is only worth having if you can have a ceiling at least 10 metres high. This avoids claustrophobia. I would also have swivel chairs so that everyone could face each other for conversation – something which you cannot get in a cinema with their fixed seats. I would also have a wonderful bar on either side of the cinema so that at any one time I could get a cold drink or a cocktail. And, of course, there should be a freezer stuffed with marvellous ice-creams – and a soft ice-cream mixer, complete with cones and flakes. And, most important of all, no downlights whatsoever in the cinema.

How would you design a massage room in one's home?

I would want it to be in a proper room with a window and not, as usually found, in a basement cell devoid of natural light with an uninviting clinical bed in the middle with bare walls and a pile of towels and bottles of oils in the corner. Rather, the room should be decorated like a small drawing room or library, with proper pieces of furniture and preferably a fireplace and a clock that tick-tocks like a therapeutic metronome. The best time for a massage is just before sunset, with the fading amber filling the room. That's why a massage room ought to have a west-facing window, a detail which always seems to escape slovenly designers. As dusk sets in, the massage room descends into darkness and a couple of candles (and the fire if appropriate) would be lit.

With twilight, the room would glow with flickering flames and playing softly in the background would be one of Schubert's last piano sonatas or Debussy's string quartet. At the end of the massage, the dimmer lights should be turned up and one would have a drink of water and then perhaps something stiffer from a tray of drinks on the side. Slouch into an armchair and relax further in semi-darkness when I might have the poem 'Prufrock' coming through the speakers. But absolutely no television, which is an invitation to mindlessness. Then in an en suite bathroom, a gentle shower or, even better, a hot steam with eucalyptus essence. So a massage room is one in which we should spend time. Make sure, however, that the masseuse is good. There is absolutely no point fussing over all the decorations and ending up with a pair of palms which does not pressurize the right points of nerves or plough over the correct contour of muscles.

Is a bar acceptable in a home? It is almost ubiquitous in America, but there seems to be a rise in their existence in England, especially in London where expensive flats are installing them as if it is de rigueur.

Dreadful. A bar is commercial and having one at home would be equivalent to having a lectern with a reservation book by the door of the dining room. The only thing I would do to a bar is to bar it. But new monies love it because they consider it conducive to 'mates' having easy conversations around it. They might be forgiven for replicating what they see in Hollywood movies in which the bar is seen to be abundant in American homes, but it looks right only because it is in a movie!

What is wrong with a simple silver tray on which are found just a few choice bottles and glasses, instead of the vulgarity of a full complement of drinks and dangling inverted glasses reminiscent of a pub? The answer is nothing, and it is considerably less crass.

I write this to you from afar, being on the south-west coast of Western Australia, from the seaside city of Mandurah. I note with interest the bit about the subject of bars in homes. Perhaps the best and maybe even the most stylish way in which to both keep one's liquors and serve them to guests would be in a beautiful art deco cocktail cabinet.

Art deco is one of those styles which is hard to mix and match unlike, say, the classical and the avant-garde, or the Gothic and art nouveau.

Accordingly, for a beautiful art deco cocktail cabinet to look right, it has to stand in a room filled only with art deco furniture, all Jeeves and Woosterish. So do you have that in your home tucked away in that obscure corner of Western Australia? Would your neighbours be able to appreciate your art deco elegance? I am surprised that you are serving martinis when surely cocktail glasses alone would be a little too delicate and effeminate for you Crocodile Dundees? I would expect men down under to siphon off only beer, or gallons of it. I, along with many readers I am sure, would defer to hear from you on all the subtle etiquette of libation in the middle of suburban Western Australia.

Swimming pools come in all forms, shapes and sizes. What would you consider to be the perfect pool? And would you have it in black, which seems to be the trend?

Adrian Zecha, my genius friend who started the Aman group at the ripe old age of 55, popularized swimming pools with black tiles at his house in Bali and villas at Amanpuri. These black pools exude a distinct sense of Zen and, under swaying palms on balmy afternoons, they represent the best of oriental tranquillity and romance. But somehow, black pools look incongruous in the West, in say, the South of France. It's like having sweet-and-sour pork for lunch at Cinquante-Cinq in St Tropez.

On shapes, I hate anything amoebic. It's very Surrey to have irregular lines for a pool. Much safer not to reinvent the wheel and, instead, keep the pool rectangular, with the longer side for laps. The perfect size would be Olympic size (55 yards I think) so that one could appreciate how slow one is compared with the likes of Mark Spitz, whose moustache must have caused a bit of a drag.

BEDROOM

Where do you stand on bed styling? Do you favour the piled-on textured cushion and layered bedspread/throw look or something more minimal? I wonder if this trend is just a ruse to get me to part with more cash when simple linen would suffice.

My wife and I believe that our house is run for the sole comfort and convenience of our dogs. So we have a large throw over our bed specifically for our two puppies, a Westie and a Jack Russell, as well as our grandfather Westie who is nearly 16. There is hardly any room for cushions, which shouldn't belong on a bed anyway. I particularly object to large square ones placed in a diamond shape as decorative pieces. They look phoney.

Save your money and leave your bed alone with its linen, so that you can conveniently get into and out of it without having to 'make it up' or 'turn it down', like a hotel room. Only pretentious people would go out to buy bedspreads, often vulgarly elaborate ones with the ghastly neo-classical Versace look, as if they need to cover beds up to make bedrooms look 'grander' or 'neat and tidy' – not dissimilar to having an ugly cabinet made in order to hide a television set, which is pointless. These are moronic practices derived from the pathetic notion of hotel designers that a bedroom looks better without a bed or a television set. How contrived and impractical!

I am thinking of consciously uncoupling from my original mattress, which has become lumpy – can you recommend a luxurious mattress maker for coupledom?

I am amused by the topical phrase 'conscious uncoupling' you have cleverly applied to your mattress. I'm not sure, however, if the delectable Gwyneth Paltrow and her uncoupling spouse, pop icon Chris Martin, would be flattered by the comparison. Just imagine being a mattress and having this glamorous couple on top every night! How they have made their mattress metaphorically lumpy is probably not comprehensible to most of us mortals untouched by Hollywood stardom. For your own relatively mundane mattress, I would suggest you simply turn it over. This method of sleeping on the original bottom side should do the trick. If you've already turned your mattress or are determined to replace it, then you must think, given 'conscious uncoupling', whether you should have one new big mattress or two new connecting mattresses, rather than worry about what brand. My wife complains that I move too much at night and prefers two mattresses, albeit zipped up along the centre seam. But this could become a classic trap for one's elbow to sink into, with scenarios evocative of Inspector Clouseau, which does not make it ideal for seduction. Safer, therefore, to have one big mattress.

LIVING ROOM

What is your view about pieces of furniture in leather at home? I have noticed more of them, especially in new homes. Is this a new trend?

Leather armchairs and sofas are beyond the pale in one's home – unless they are at least 50 years old and well worn. Otherwise, they should only be found in the front or the back of a car. Particularly nasty is leather in black, and laughable attempts at distressing those cheap samples to make them look antique. The police should be called to arrest the trend. One must be careful not to give evidence by saying that leather smells, as Dr Johnson reminded us that we smell, and things stink. Only Rolls-Royces should be allowed black leather, because they use the Connolly brand which exudes a scent of luxuriance that intensifies over the years. I feel as if I'm a glue-sniffer whenever I slide into a Flying Spur or a Silver Shadow.

Would you regard a fireplace with a real fire essential in a home? Or do you prefer central heating all round so that you don't have to be bothered by anything other than a thermostat?

I regard a real fireplace as the height of luxury in any home, modest or grand. It is one of the best inventions of the West in interior decorations. We Chinese had the 'kang', which was a bed heated from underneath with the fire out of sight. Thereafter, we never progressed to any naked flames, which have to be one of the greatest comforting sights in the cold. Any country house without a real fire is not worth having, no matter how charming, delightful or grand it is.

In London, there are restrictions on burning logs, which are the best fuel, but gas is not such a bad substitute as long as there is a flame flickering and giving out heat. In the cold there is no greater luxury than sitting next to a fire, perhaps having a crumpet with melted butter and jam and a builder's strength cuppa, reading a book or having conversations with others or even, God forbid, looking at one's iPhone or Black-Berry. The ultimate is, however, to have a roaring fire in front of a bath, or to sleep with another in a bedroom with a fire's shimmering shadows as if one was James Bond with his belle de jour! So forget about dreaded central heating with its ugly metallic grilles, or underfloor heating, which is too hygienic and clever by half.

There seems to be a growing consensus that it is in fine taste to hang a flat-screen television over a fireplace. Something about this trend has always struck me as tacky, though I can't say I can really put my finger on why. Perhaps it's because in the past that space often served as a location for an important object, such as a painting or a sword. Am I being ridiculous?

It seems to be very common now, especially in the US, even among the super-rich. It is indeed exceedingly common to hang a flat screen over a fireplace, and doubly naff if it were to be a working fireplace. Imagine a roaring fire – one of the most warming and comforting aspects to enhance a room – being distracted immediately above by vulgar advertisements in between mindless games and soaps or gratuitous violent movies. A flat screen above a fireplace also anchors it as the centre of gravity in the room, which says a great deal about the wanton relegation of books and conversations that are the very linchpin of civilization.

And you are right about the TV being a very poor substitute for a proper painting, although you might be wrong that a sword should ever be hung above a fireplace, unless you had thousands of them and they could be arranged magnificently, as in the Sword Room at St James's Palace. I don't have a collection of swords but I do have a great variety of flick knives, which I have arranged in a large glass case that hangs in the hallway to my set at Albany. I think it suggests masculine street cred.

As for the super-rich, or more to the point, the *nouveaux riches*, they seem to hang as many big flat screens as they can all over their vast houses, whether or not there are fireplaces. The proof of this comes from the endless pages of *Hello!* magazine in which the homes of so-called 'celebrities' are consumed in the background by flat screens – in the kitchen, sitting room, dining room, 'study', bedroom and even bathrooms. It is all a bit pathetic if one thinks they could all be substituted and better enhanced by a small Roberts wireless set that is easily taken from room to room, gently issuing intelligent programmes from Radio 4 or wonderful music from Radio 3 or even titillating gems from Classic FM.

A friend of mine has a white grand piano placed in his drawing room, with the lid permanently open, even though nobody in the family plays the instrument. The keyboard, however, has one of those automatic machines that functions like a pianola. When switched on, a Chopin nocturne or a ragtime by Joplin springs to sound. Acceptable or not?

I cannot think of anything more unacceptable. For a start, you can only have a white piano if you are either Liberace or John Lennon, who were both over the top – Liberace with air-conditioning in his garden through which he walked in his heavily sequined white tie; and Lennon going around naked with Yoko Ono and hanging a Dalí above his lavatory. Otherwise, all pianos should be in black, preferably a nine-foot Steinway or that Bösendorfer with three phantom white keys in black at the bass for perfect balance.* A Chopin nocturne or ragtime by Joplin should always be avoided because they are plebeian and excruciating if they ring out of a modern pianola. The piano is not a piece of furniture, nor should it be camouflaged as a hi-fi; it is a beautiful instrument that demands to be played. Unless you inherit one or play one, you should not have one, any more than you should have a double-bass or a French horn hung up on the wall as sconces.

In his footnote to your column yesterday, Ed [*Who he? Ed.*] alleges that you 'tinkle' the plastics on an electronic keyboard (as opposed to the ivories on a piano). Surely he means 'tickle'.

First of all, Ed. stands for editor. Have you never read *Private Eye*? Second, my editor is a woman and not a man. Third, the predicate is always 'tinkle' and never 'tickle', ivories or not. Therefore, you are ignorant on the first count; presumptuous on your second; and uneducated on your third. Anything else?

* In the interests of editorial accuracy I have to reveal that, despite David Tang's highfalutin answer, he tinkles the plastics on a utilitarian electronic keyboard while entertaining at his Hyde Park residence. Ed.**

** In the interest of space, my Bösendorfer is at my house at Eaton Terrace and too big for my garden chapel. D. Tang.

DINING ROOM

I wonder what you think about stemless wine glasses. When Riedel came out with a stemless goblet, I bought some and have seldom used stems since. Yes, it's lovely to see tall glassware on the table. But then there are the shrieks as a knocked-over glass of red goes flying, everyone jumping up to save their outfits – invariably white – plus the conversation-killing mop-up, the anguish of the knocker-over, etc.

The Riedel stemless wine goblet is foul to look at and fouler to drink wine from. Calling it a 'goblet' is an insult to me as a good Catholic altar boy who is used to gleaming silver grails at Mass. If you are so antsy about wine glasses having stems, you should get some old ones without stems – especially those with a square crystal base. The idea that you should worry endlessly about glasses of red wine being knocked over is typically one of those irritating middle-class anxieties best consigned to oblivion. If a glass of red wine is knocked over, then it's knocked over. We will just have to clean it up. Blotches on table-cloths and carpets are the marks of stylish nonchalance and confidence.

What is your position on using place mats and coasters to protect tables from the marks made by plates and glasses?

They are usually made of ersatz leather or cork. I think they are horrible and result in more food and liquid being spilled than if they hadn't been used at all.

Unless the surface is an original Chippendale or better, it is too precious, and therefore bourgeois, to use mats and coasters. It is, however, marginally less bad than asking people to take off their shoes for the carpet or the floor at home, and as bad as decanting Blue Nun.

Should a magnificently long mahogany table always be covered by a white tablecloth? Is any other colour tablecloth permissible? Or are there circumstances in which only table mats should be used?

It is acceptable, at breakfast, to use table mats rather than a full long tablecloth. It is how the table is set at a typical shooting breakfast, with the broadsheets and tabloids spreading themselves over the butter and marmalade. But at dinner, with candles lit and curtains drawn opposite a glowing log fire, a crisply ironed white tablecloth is an indispensable part of a visual feast. White is de rigueur, except perhaps with a piece of over-washed and over-starched damask in beige. I possess a perfect example of this from old Australia, if that is not an oxymoron. The truth is that the stature of a long tablecloth is defined by its stiffness through starching and the prominence of its creases. One of the most puzzling questions under which I have laboured for years and to which I have yet to meet anyone able to provide a cogent answer is: how did Leonardo da Vinci manage to paint, in his *Last Supper*, the long tablecloth with immaculate creases in perfect rectangles? I can't quite believe that people ironed table-cloths in AD 33, when Jesus Christ had his last meal. Or was it, inconceivably, already a bourgeois practice by the 15th century when Leonardo lived? If old Leonardo was offering verisimilitude, how did people manage to obtain the beautiful creases? It is a practical fact that you cannot fold anything more than seven times, and presses and mangle boards and flat irons didn't come into use in Europe until the 18th century, even though I believe we clever Chinese were using pan irons on fabrics as early as the 12th century. But we didn't have a Leonardo Wong!

FOLIAGE

House plants – surely these triffids, bringing the aura of bell bottoms and patchouli, are outdated and unacceptable (unless they are, of course, blowsy blossoms brought in for weekends from a vast greenhouse).

Somehow, I have always immediately associated house plants with university digs, and I can almost see them in my mind's eye by the windowsills of every female undergraduate room. When the cheap curtains are drawn, the small struggling plant is always in focus as one lies in bed smoking a mindless cigarette. I would remember a line or two from my favourite Irish poet Louis MacNeice: '. . . The first train passes and the windows groan . . .'

But you mention the triffids that are, of course, a fictional plant invented by John Wyndham. As a young boy, I read with trepidation *The Day of the Triffids* and innocently asked to see them on my first visit to Kew because I thought only a large greenhouse like that would have been able to accommodate their height.

What are your views about flowers in the home? Should they only be fresh? Are artificial bouquets ever acceptable?

Plastic flowers should only be used as part of a deliberate kitsch design. Sometimes it is amusing to have kitsch, although there is always good kitsch and bad kitsch. But I have never written off plastic flowers as a total joke, because it is a well-known fact that Li Ka-shing, the richest man in Asia, started his business with plastic flowers and therefore they must have good feng shui! As for other types of artificial flowers, I only like the ones in glass, because they look like works of art.

But nothing beats freshly cut flowers, and I would only want them in their normal blooming seasons. So daffodils and tulips in spring, although Holland now produces tulips all year round and, worse, some stained with artificial colours. That's bad news. Equally bad news is when arrangements similar to those found in hotels are used at home. Bouquets tightly bunched together look sterile and inanimate.

I was always impressed by what Mark Birley put around his home and in his clubs. The flowers were always gathered together with abandon in perfect clashing colours. And I have never found any florist in London able to offer bouquets that come anywhere near them. There are now fewer and fewer florists in the capital and their gradual disappearance is because of a lack of aesthetics, or high rents, or both. Thankfully, there are some florists, like my friend Flora Starkey, who are creative, using uncommon plants and flowers and attempting to recreate the sumptuous arrangements seen in old Dutch paintings. Extraordinarily, the originators of this movement came from Brooklyn. It is high time New York's Upper East Side grandees started taking note that most of the flower arrangements in their houses are not what well-to-do people should be proud of. I do hope the imagination of florists will re-emerge and bring about a renaissance of flowers and their arrangements.

I was wondering what your thoughts are on silk flowers?

There is one type of flower worse than silk flowers and it is plastic flowers. Both of these types are infra dig because they pretend to be what they are not, ie fresh and real flowers. So dried flowers are just about all right because at least they have half a life of naturalness. But this does not mean that all fresh flowers are necessarily acceptable. When they are arranged in a contrived or pretentious manner, they are as bad. Particularly if all of the colours were to clash, or the selection of flowers blindly put together.

There is virtually no place in London where flowers are arranged better than all those establishments created by the late Mark Birley. He had a real eye for what looked right, with a stylish sense of abandon.

I cannot see how flowers can 'clash' in colour. Mother Nature does not discriminate and one of the rare joys in life is to see a riot of colour in a field of wild flowers. While I agree that any artificial flower is horrible, to me even worse is using out-of-season flowers in an arrangement. Chrysanthemums are for the autumn, phlox for summer and tulips for spring.

Why don't you try putting together in a vase a white lily, a pink carnation, a red rose, a yellow sunflower and a purple tulip, and tell me if they do not clash. (The only acceptable 'clash' in my book is the punk group The Clash, whose lead guitarist is, I can boast, my friend Mick Jones.) But I agree with you about 'seasonal' flowers. Tulips are now readily available throughout the year, demonstrating a sense of arrogance against nature.

Worst of all is the way the Dutch, clutching on to their provenance of Van Gogh, started dyeing the tulip into different colours. Maybe it is the flat horizons and monotonously large skies of Holland that have made them think they need to interfere with nature to make it more interesting. These Dutchmen need their minds unclogged.

• • •

Some comments you wrote a while back on some of your preferred ritualistic grace notes in taking a bath – the radio, the cigar, the whisky – prompted us to redecorate our bathroom and for me to adopt similar rituals of my own. What else is there that you have discovered that one might consider adopting into one's own routine?

The best routine is to use as much as possible all the best things we have for ourselves. I have noticed that those who are in possession of good silver and crockery and cutlery tend to save all of them up for a smart dinner party; while for their own use, they actually go out of their way to buy lesser versions. This seems to me a rather strange way of living. If I could afford good silver and crockery and cutlery, I would use them every day, especially when eating alone or *en famille*, and not save them for guests. Another excellent routine is to have a properly starched napkin of a good size – even, or especially, at breakfast or teatime. A beautifully crisp napkin makes eating exceptionally civilized.

TECHNOLOGY

'Is the use of a concealed electronic jammer acceptable
if one's dining partner is glued to their iPhone?'

J UST AS WE have had our lives fundamentally changed by the internet and mobile phones over the past two decades, so too must we brace ourselves for further seismic shifts to come, courtesy of the imminent impact of robots and artificial intelligence (AI). The appropriate phrase must now be 'stranger than science fiction'.

Robots have been on the rise – perhaps without our realization. Already in America, there are 10 robots for every 1,000 human labourers, while in Germany the figure is 28, in Japan 32 and in South Korea 40 – and each of these numbers is increasing. In China, the density currently stands at 3 robots per 1,000 workers, but here too the figure is growing at an exponential rate. By 2020 it is estimated that China will have 800,000 robots, replacing a workforce of 3.5 million. There can be no doubt that this will bring about far-reaching consequences in society and economics, completely overhauling the way in which we interact with one another and posing all manner of new social dilemmas.

Already there are restaurants run by technology: customers order online, they are shown to designated tables by computers, and their food and drinks are dispensed by robots. Consider how we are already obsessed with looking at our mobile devices in restaurants, rather than talking to each other; soon people eating out in restaurants might not engage in any human interactions at all! And technology could well create more silences in our lives. Taken to its outer limits, we could get up and have breakfast already prepared for us, go to work in a driverless car, train or bus, and sit in an office full of computers and robots and AI. All the while we would have no need for any kind of audible interaction, and so it would continue until we get home, eat our pre-prepared dinner, watch television and go to bed. It is easy to imagine how our daily routine could be at best eerily quiet, or indeed utterly silent.

In AI, there are new discoveries and inventions each day. Mirroring Garry Kasparov's famous defeat by the chess-playing computer Deep Blue, more recently a computer program developed by Google managed to beat the world champion of the ancient game of Go. The driverless car now seems less a fantastical prospect than an inevitable part of the near future, and many other extraordinary things will alter further the way in which we live. The world of science fiction, in which machines can think with intuition and make free decisions, is no longer so distant from our own. AI could identify products we might need and order them online; match us with potential partners on dating services; suggest meals we might never think of eating, or holidays we might never dream of having. It could enrich our own imagination to a degree we would never have thought possible. But how do we respond to the new social situations this will present to us, whether human-to-human or human-to-machine?

Consider a world in which inanimate machines are taking over the decision-making processes from us, animate human beings. This would definitely alter the way we think and choose and behave. It could even challenge the whole Darwinian theory of natural selection. Might AI eventually supplant the human species as the top dog in nature? We really must heed what AI is capable of doing! Remember the film *2001: A Space Odyssey*? The computer HAL 9000 was clever enough on its own to perfect the technique of lip-reading, and used the skill to discover that the two astronauts on board had discussed the possibility of disconnecting it because they thought it was beginning to make mistakes. So HAL set out to pre-empt their action by trying to murder both of them, by shutting them out and not re-opening the hatch door to the mothership. If such an AI does not exist now, it surely will soon. That's the advancing world towards which we, like Mr Spock, are made 'to boldly go where no man has gone before'!

MOBILE PHONES

The use of the BlackBerry or iPhone is now so common that in restaurants one can see that general conversations are virtually substituted by individuals silently checking their devices. Is such antisocial behaviour a good or a bad thing?

I'd say it's an excellent thing if everyone round the table is a right bore. I have been to too many lunches and dinners at which people's conversations are totally resistible, and now we have the secret weapon of not having to listen to them but, instead, do our own thing by making excuses for having to deal with emergencies, real or otherwise.

But it's obviously a bad thing if one is trying to engage others in conversation or to impress someone in business or, even more so, someone whom one fancies. Sometimes I carry with me a secret electronic jammer that is concealed inside what looks like an ordinary book. My own dust cover is bespoken to *Biggles in the Orient*, a story of how the Japanese practised sabotage by injecting a drug into the chewing gums that were dispensed to all RAF pilots. Once they started chewing, they became disorientated in the sky and crashed. By placing such a book innocently on the table, all the mobiles are jammed and it is sometimes hilarious to see the general panic it causes. Then everyone is forced to revert to the good old days when a repast was treated as an enjoyable occasion when decent conversations took place.

But in the absence of a mischievous jammer, there seems to be no stopping the overwhelming use of the mobile in one form or another. My physiotherapist tells me that the way in which everyone now dips their neck in order to read their texts is going to cause considerable problems, because of arterial constrictions to the flow of blood to the brain. Not to mention all sorts of elbow, hand and finger fatigue through their constant use.

The truth is that we are developing detrimental changes to our health without being conscious of their seriousness. Maybe in time, humans will evolve with an extra-long neck like a crane, and perhaps an extra-long finger like the mysterious Madagascan aye-aye.

At mealtimes nowadays, be it breakfast, lunch, dinner or even just having a cup of tea, we seem no longer able to resist using our iPhones, Samsungs or BlackBerrys. Is this antisocial practice going to continue or even get worse? Are those who complain simply fuddy-duddies who are lagging behind the times and need to get wise and accept this dramatic change in our social behaviour?

Alas, it is a sorrowful sight that, even at home, families now seem incapable of getting through a repast without cyber interference. Parents now cannot tell their children off for using their devices because they themselves use them. Father is looking at all his business messages and perhaps escapades with his mates or even rendezvous with a mistress or girlfriend; mother is making dates with her lover, or gossiping with her girlfriends about facelifts and her husband's money; the daughter is Instagramming her own pictures, looking at others, and obsessing about new boyfriends or pop idols; and the son is joshing with his pals, looking at porn sites, or gaming. Dinner is no longer a gathering of people eating, but an assembly of family members talking silently among themselves individually.

It is no different in any restaurant. I bet you will always find more than half of the customers using their mobile devices at any one time, even couples eating à deux. Most tragic of all is when even brief interludes, such as getting into or out of a plane, car or boat, are now used up with our eyes half-trained on our devices. Ditto for walking in the street, crossing the road, waiting in a queue or even inside a cinema – we are now all plagued by our mobile gadgets.

I fear this dramatic change in our social behaviour is much, much greater than we are willing to admit and it will not let up. On the contrary, more and more people are going to go round acting like zombies, believing that they cannot live without checking their devices, which have begun to rule their lives. I think we should start categorizing modern mobile zombies. For a start, I might nominate my wife and two children for having been zombified. They probably regard me as a zombie as well, although in my opinion I am, at worst, only a half-zombie. But it will be a good game for readers to play: identifying mobile zombies in our modern times. I suspect there are billions of them.

A dear friend and consummate host to some memorable dinner parties has solved the electronic zombification plague that his guests cannot wean themselves off: he has purchased a mobile-phone blocker (likely illegal) from an online firm in China, which obliterates mobile signals. His guests are mystified as to why they have no reception and must wander 100 yards from his kitchen/dining area if they want to engage in their connected addiction.

It is indeed a good trick to get an electronic jammer and hide it in order to stop offenders, especially at dinner parties. It can be very amusing. More so if one takes one on to a train, just to see some passengers freaking out.

But I would suggest a much more effective method. Just buy

a house in rural Wales, Devon, the Yorkshire Dales or Northumberland. There is usually no signal to be found in large parts of rural Britain. Whenever I go shooting at these places, even in Oxfordshire, I cannot get a signal. It is more archaic than many third-world countries where signals are strong even in deserts and on mountains.

I've never understood why the UK government does not insist that any successful bidder for mobile wavebands has to align the entire area of their influence with a grid of transponders, irrespective of population density. This way, the whole country would be covered. In Hong Kong, we have superb coverage. Even underground and in tunnels, the signal is strong for yapping Cantonese who love talking loudly.

A friend of mine was visiting when her mobile rang in the middle of our conversation. She answered it and I could hear some of the words from the caller while I was trying to pretend it didn't matter. When the call ended, instead of giving me an indication of the importance of the call, she passed on to another subject and soon made for the exit. What do you think?

It is indeed a sad state of affairs when the telephone/BlackBerry/iPhone have now invaded our daily lives so unforgivingly. There is no airport or aircraft, no train station or train, no ferry terminal or ferry, no park or street or alleyway at which zombie-like characters are not listening to, or speaking on, or reading their cyber devices. Even when I am sitting at a beautiful Parisian café on a beautiful spring morning, I will see, *mon dieu*, Parisians doing the same! The most interesting consequence from this rather depressing observation is that I can now pick out the left-handers without difficulty. It's the kind of empiricism that would have pleased even Locke. I can also imagine Descartes arguing for '*Emailo, Ergo Sum*'!

It is indeed irritating when someone with whom we are having a conversation suddenly switches to an incoming call. They might say sorry because it's their sick mother or lie about other sympathetic stories. But they are seldom contrite. Otherwise, they would not have taken the call in the first place. Even worse is when you are having lunch or dinner with those who surreptitiously divert their gaze on to their lap, or blatantly carry on reading their messages.

To deal with this new antisocial behaviour, I simply walk away without explanation. This usually rattles them as they half try to continue their conversation, and half try to apologize with some frantic gesticulation. That's what you should have done to your friend – in mid-flow of her call, you turn your back on her in silence and disappear into the sunset.

By far the worst behaviour is when a phone rings in the middle of an artistic performance. I saw a marvellous clip on YouTube when, at precisely the critical pause in a concerto, that familiar sugary tune of a mobile rang out in the audience. The solo violinist was visibly flabbergasted. But without a moment's hesitation, he suddenly played on his violin an echo of the appalling tune.

TECHNOLOGY IN THE HOME

A lot of my friends seem to be very fussy about the sound system in their homes. Normal speakers in stereo seem to have been overtaken by at least a set of four speakers offering what is generally known as 'surround-sound'. Some will go further with speakers installed in several rooms of the house with individual remote controls. What are your views?

I have always fantasized about using one of those 'touch-screen' remote-control panels to amplify my voice so that I could utter some primeval scream of frustration and have it piped through the speakers. Indeed, isn't it pathetic that those designers of remote controls can contrive a kaleidoscopic collection of functions and yet never install a simple speaker function – which would be exceedingly useful at home for summoning one's child to bring along one's slippers?

Instead, the panel is replete with options, one more convoluted than the next, and I am forever negotiating my way through them. Worst of all is when their champions, who are irritating nerds, begin showing off to their guests about how 'amazing' and 'incredible' their audio system is. At these tiresome demonstrations, I will cut them short and ask if they know of the range of frequencies that a human ear can detect. 'Twenty hertz to twenty kilohertz? And how about the infrasound and the ultrasound?' I ask nonchalantly. Of course they will be foxed by a remark like that and it is enjoyable to see them wrong-footed. The scientific truth is that the human ear, especially for an ageing male, is not particularly sensitive in picking out the high frequencies, unlike, say, bats or dolphins. So when very expensive amplifiers and speakers are being offered to you by pressing salesmen who drone on about sensitive pitches, they are trying to flog you frequencies indiscernible by the human ear and therefore pointless. Sometimes it's not even enjoyable to hear a voice in all its sharpness, just as television screens offer high-definition images that, paradoxically, appear plastic and surreal.

I am afraid we live in an age of what I might call technological affectations. So-called experts will invariably throw around designs in order to show off software that in reality is redundant. They have no common sense of design or purpose. They are the perpetuators of confusions, doing us a great disservice by wrongly jamming into our lives superfluous inventions that are dysfunctional. What we have to do is to resist all of their patters and banters, and choose for ourselves something easy and simple, except that these easy and simple things are now virtually impossible to find!

Should everything nowadays be operated by remote controls? Aren't they a modern invention to behold?

No, and I would like to kill all those people who 'design' remote controls. Why do they have to make them so complicated? The worst are those touch-screen 'monitors' which are so heavy and convoluted that they need to be permanently powered in a tray of charging electricity. When they are taken out, I never quite seem to find the option I want and invariably end up tapping on the screen furiously. The result is a fuzzy screen which takes ages to rectify, thereby defeating the whole purpose of the remote control.

As for wall panels in hotels, they are all designed by idiots who have no idea about human eyesight as the instructions are always too small to read. We all end up kissing these wretched panels and screwing up our eyes to find out what's what. So unnecessary and undignified.

What are your thoughts on 'smart' refrigerators, which will text their owners when it is time to replenish, say, the Riesling? With this 'internet of things', it seems it won't be long until every appliance is configured to annoy us with warnings.

Technology is always on the march and we should all embrace its advances. Recently, I was checking out of a hotel when I volunteered that I had taken a bottle of Evian out of the fridge. The receptionist smiled and said: 'We know.' But how? 'The moment you pick up a bottle in the fridge,' came the reply, 'our computer picks up the information.' It was a disconcerting feeling because I wondered what else they might have discovered by remote control in the privacy of my room.

I just wanted to say how much your observation about the proliferation of ever larger flat screens in domestic homes resonated. In terms of antisocial behaviour, do their owners ever turn them off or reduce the volume when you visit?

The most nauseous welcome is when one arrives at a home where a bored child is using a large flat screen to play some sadistic computer game, with loud electronic noises, and not looking up in the slightest to acknowledge another's presence. Worse still is when neither parent makes any attempt to make the child learn basic manners.

The sadness of the modern family home is now dominated by the internet and social media, and the appalling, yet bursting, industry of mindless computer games. Soon babies will be born with a crooked neck and the nimblest of fingers. Perish the thought of reading bedtime stories to children, as they will be surfing the net, chatting with friends on their iPhones, or killing virtual dragons on screen. At mealtimes, conversations will be hijacked by silences, not for monastic practise but for checking and sending electronic messages. The flat screen will become ever larger until, one day, IMAX screens will be installed in drawing rooms and bedrooms. Kenneth Clark would be spinning like a dervish in his grave over such 'progress' in civilization.

Are mechanical clocks going out of fashion? Do you think they will soon become obsolete and be replaced by electronic ones?

I have always liked an old-fashioned mechanical clock, especially one which chimes with a pendulum. That tick-tock sound in the silence of a room is magically soothing, and a perfect backdrop to reading a good book or a prelude to a slumber. The only drawback of a mechanical clock is that it requires winding regularly and a few calibrations to keep good time. There is nothing more annoying than a clock that has stopped, or one that goes too fast or too slow. The royal clocks at Sandringham were famously made fast by half an hour because Edward VII wanted to pretend there was more daylight for the shoots. This time warp continued through the reign of George V until Edward VIII ordered for all the clocks to show the correct time – an act which has always puzzled me because he could have seen Mrs Simpson half an hour earlier each day.

But British royalty are not the only lot who interfere with time. Uighurs in the Muslim province of Xinjiang in China continue to set their watches and clocks two hours behind the single timezone of China. It was very confusing when I wanted to find out the starting time of the Sunday livestock market in Kashgar and was told various times between six o'clock and eight o'clock. But I am sympathetic to their defiance on such a basic matter in order to demonstrate their distinct ethnicity.

The main problem with modern electronic clocks is that they are produced without any sense of craftsmanship. Most are made in cheap plastic or wood. Even expensive brands have failed to make electronic clocks desirable. And of course, worst of all, the second hand of any quartz movement is an awkward tick without a tock, which makes its entire movement a constant series of jerks – probably not unlike their owners.

In view of the ever-changing internet world, should there be design elements for homes, whether newly built or not, to anticipate a changing world of living?

I would concentrate on the bathroom and make it larger and soften it with pieces of furniture and dispense with, as much as possible, all the hard surfaces such as marble floors or tiling walls. The reason is because, increasingly, people are going to spend much more time in the bathroom using their iPods, iPhones and iPads, and BlackBerrys or laptops. Next to the lav I would put a table on which all these modern devices can be placed so that they don't have to go on the floor which is what usually happens nowadays. Worse is when you drop any of them on a hard surface and they break or, even more annoyingly, fall into a basin or the reservoir of the loo. Then in a corner somewhere, in compliance somehow with 'health and safety', I would have sockets for charging all the devices, not to mention simple speakers for music and other gadgets as voice recognition becomes more widely used. Adjacent to the bath I would put another table at more or less the same height so that, again, those life-ruling electronics can conveniently rest while bathing. And I'd add a hook for a dry flannel with which to wipe one's hands to make gizmo-use easy mid-bath.

But of course all of this is predicated on getting good or excellent internet access. If you can get hold of fibre optic, grab it. Any place which has poor reception is fast becoming a turn-off for people. Country-house guests now regard WiFi as more important than staff, and if there is ineffectual WiFi, hosts will find a dwindling number of guests. For commercial ventures such as a rented shoot, it is now of paramount importance that there are decent signals and automatic WiFi everywhere so that in between drives, executives can check communications, however trivial.

As time goes by, more and more aspects of our lives will interact with cyberspace: groceries will be routinely ordered online, and other purchases will continue to infest our homes. All of this will be regarded as an improved way of living. If you read the latest book by the two world experts on the internet, Eric Schmidt and Jared Cohen, you will be able to imagine an extraordinary version of an ordinary day in which most of us will go about our business radically changed, starting with getting up not to an alarm clock but to the smell of coffee and having had a perfect night's sleep through some electronic device placed underneath the mattress.

What bothers me is whether such a day is the kind of perfect routine we would like to have. Wouldn't we get bored by it? For me, I don't want regimentation. The problem with any electronic devices is that they need to be set beforehand, yet I don't want to decide what I wish to do until I feel like doing something. I might want to go for a jog or go round to my corner shop for the papers and say 'hello' to Mr Singh and talk to him about cricket. It all sounds a bit old-fogey and fuddy-duddy I know, but I also know that internet fatigue, given the irrational nature of the human race, will set in much sooner than we think. I certainly hope so, because a world of superficial and genuine nerds is not one I crave. Thankfully, none of the implications of the internet which entails a dramatic rise in connectivity will touch on the likes of genius concert pianists or champion athletes or dedicated craftsmen, all of whose obsessions cannot be accelerated by even the most powerful internet.

INTERNET

You once said that you did not trust the likes of TripAdvisor, so how do you select the hotels at places you have never been to?

I google every image available of each hotel in the area and immediately discard those that look totally ghastly, which is usually an easy task. Then I eventually settle for the least bad one, or the best of the good ones, again by pure instinct. But looking for hotels might soon become a habit of the past. The trend, and it is a very fast moving trend, is that of travellers, especially younger ones, looking to stay in private bed-and-breakfast accommodation. They want to soak up the local flavours and eat and live like the local residents of the place they are visiting. They are also fed up with the tediously homogeneous look of so many hotels with their stale starred ranking. Websites such as Airbnb have already made a vast difference to the travel pattern of the world and this will grow probably exponentially.

Given the internet revolution, shouldn't you extend your advice column to cover privacy as well as questions of properties and proprieties? What are the new protocols? How should one greet someone wearing Google glasses?

I am not at all optimistic about any new protocols in our fast-expanding cyber universe, as they all seem destined towards maximum tolerance for antisocial behaviour. Take privacy – there has clearly been an invasion. Almost anyone is now searchable on Google or social media sites, and anyone remotely engaged would have a Wikipedia entry, which is not unknown to be replete with inaccuracies.

Once at a reception, I was waylaid by someone who asked me about 'my' gold Rolls-Royce with an extension in which a lavatory had been installed. I was quick to point out that the ownership of the converted monstrosity belonged to another 'David Tang', a native of Taipei.

For properties, it is now essential to have good internet reception. But there are still many large pockets around rural Britain that are out of range of even normal mobile reception, let alone WiFi. The question becomes: would you buy a property, however attractive, if you knew full well

**that your mobile phone will not work in it, or where there is
no broadband and WiFi?**

Those living in internet-deprived areas are clearly at a disadvantage in our age of instant information. They might well be the
last to know about a third world war or a nuclear wipeout. Some
of them might have to be resigned to living out the pathos and
romance of the last couple on earth in Nevil Shute's *On the Beach*.

Regarding proprieties, the invasion of hand devices has dramatically made day-to-day life irksome. At restaurants, tedious
monologues and mono-screening have overtaken human conversations and interactions. When something rings or pings, the
worst offenders put their hands across the table to command
silence and then, unsatisfied, leave the table to continue a call. It
seems that priority in mobile usage has usurped propriety in
basic manners. Even at home, particularly at breakfast or dinner, young people dip their heads to check their messages or
Facebooks or Twitters or Instagrams, as if they are a matter of
life and death. The intrusion of cyber waves in our everyday living seems to be turning most of us into zombies. The final straw
would be if we all went round wearing Google glasses so that in
whatever we were doing, we would at the same time be Google-
searching in the corner of our vision. This obsession with the
internet reminds me of that marvellous 1973 science-fiction
movie *Westworld*, in which Yul Brynner went around with a
bionic eye. It all went pear-shaped, of course.

**In the age of the internet, there are more and more
inventions which someone like me – unfamiliar with
computer technology – finds increasingly baffling and hard
to execute. Must we resign ourselves to the fact that if we
don't make the effort to keep up, we will slip more and
more out of touch with the modern world and lose out?**

I am not at all computer literate. I have never been able to grasp the use of a mouse, nor half the symbols on a screen, let alone all the operational procedures. It took me a long time to understand how to work a mobile phone and eventually its texting facility. Then when I finally worked out how to use a Black-Berry, I thought I had become gadget savvy, only to discover that every new model became more complicated and again beyond my grasp. To this day, I have resisted the iPhone because my fat fingers don't seem to be able to cope with the lettering on a touch screen. And I am continually baffled by those endless 'apps' that can do almost anything. The most ingenious is the one which, when one holds a phone to music, can trace the name of the tune within a couple of seconds. I just find that extraordinary. So we fossils must persevere with keeping up as best we can with the marching technologies of our age, and marvel at the dexterity of the younger generation, which seems to soak up new computing inventions with such ease. The only comfort I draw is that when I was a teenager, I memorized chunks of Shakespeare and poetry by heart. I can still recite most of them, whereas I have never met a teenager today who can recite anything. They just laugh and say that there is no reason to commit anything to memory because they can simply google it with the touch of a finger. Of course this is a terrible confusion of information and knowledge, which is the price we pay for all the cyber advances of our times.

SOCIAL MEDIA

Instagram – what is it if not a vehicle for the insanely thin, over-waxed and self-obsessed? I want to join a social media site but am not sure why I want to. Are you on Instagram?

It is unfathomable why anyone would want to spend an inordinate amount of time on Instagrams. First, it is frivolous: although nothing wrong with that per se, its daily volume trivializes everything and becomes tedious very soon.

Second, why post photographs that always stand impoverished against words? Third, Instagrams have become an antisocial disease. In restaurants, people don't talk any more but bury their heads into the screens of their electronic devices, trawling through tiny coloured prints. Couples sit at their table not looking at each other but into their own laps of illumination.

Worst is when one pretends to be engaged in conversation, but keeps throwing furtive glances at an electronic device held in a palm. That's why I love my clever jammer, concealed in an innocuous-looking hardback, which I casually leave and activate on the table. Instagrammers instantly go berserk, as if they are running amok in a padded cell. It is a spectacle more entertaining than watching Ben-Hur in a chariot as his wheels are spiked by the hidden spurs of his nefarious competitors.

I am a new fan of Twitter and am gutted that you are apparently not on Twitter. I am amused by the Reverend Richard Coles, who tweets powerfully on the Stages of the Cross alongside the revelries of his dogs, his garden shed and, most recently, told me to rush outside in the middle of the night to watch the space station passing high above my home . . . why don't you?

I don't tweet because it doesn't require a fountain pen, which I love using. The Reverend Richard Coles is a shade too trendy for my Catholic taste, and completing the Stations (not Stages) of the Cross ought to require a calm spiritual state of mind rather than the hurried sense of spontaneity that Twitter urges. My friends Peter and Ann Hutley, who have shown me more kindnesses than any other English couple since I first came to England as a boy, years ago made use of their estate to map out a mini pilgrimage of the Stations of the Cross. That is what I would regard as a proper modernization of an important Catholic ceremony. Not with twits who tweet on Twitter twittering away.

• • •

I write a weekly column for an international newspaper. Typically readers will write in with questions on various personal issues and I will prescribe advice. Where possible I also try to demonstrate some knowledge of trivia and make the odd joke at the readers' expense. Recently some readers have complained that my replies contained inaccurate information, or that my attempts at humour have offended them. So far I have responded to such impertinent folk by mocking them publicly in my column. I am concerned, however, that eventually such a strategy may alienate my audience, damage the weekend readership of my employer and bring my writing career to a premature end. What should I do?

So you think you are clever in presenting this problem as your own, when you clearly mean it to apply to me? Well, you are too clever by half! You should have no cause for concern about my audience, which has been growing. I have umpteen questions in front of me angling for advice and it will take me months just to answer them. As for damaging the readership, you should know that *Schadenfreude* is a magical potion for selling newspapers, and editors love increasing their circulation. So there is no sacking in the offing; at least I don't yet see a sinking ship. If you can't stand the laughing waves of the ocean, you should get off your dinghy.

BUSINESS

*'How should one conduct business wearing
nothing but spa attire?'*

I T IS A TRUTH UNIVERSALLY acknowledged that a man in business must be in want of making money. But until relatively recently, it was also universally acknowledged that all such men made their money wearing suits. All that changed with the age of the uniformly un-uniformed yuppies, for whom the stiff formality of traditional business attire was a sign of the old guard. They made quick money and lots of it; so much so that their bosses in suits on the upper floors didn't care whether their employees put on a tie or not, so long as they knew when to go long (and short) on the bond or the gilt or the equity. And so the City became more prosperous – and noisier, with a stable of the latest Porsches, the roars of which announced the arrival of the new Establishment.

The success of these yuppies, however, proved short-lived, as the markets began to resemble casinos, with spinning derivatives and levels of debts which eventually led to the collapses of even the best-regarded institutions. But in the meantime an even greater army of young men and women had become still more efficient in making fast money. Suddenly the dot.com businesses spiralled up to the heavens, with fairy-tale figures attesting to fairy-tale valuations. Instant young billionaires were made, and as with the yuppies before them they further relaxed the rules of business dress, dispensing with the last remaining vestiges of formality altogether. A photograph of Warren Buffett in a suit, arm-in-arm with Bill Gates in jeans and trainers, became the symbolic juxtaposition of the old and the young, and the old and the new.

And how about the informality of language? To my mind there can be no doubt that boardroom vocabulary has become more casual and informal in the past decade or so. As our means of communication have become ever more immediate, the formalities of language have been discarded in favour of a new and often baffling form of linguistic shorthand. This truly is the age of the abbreviation, with offices across the world reverberating to the staccato rhythm of impenetrable terms such as VPN, EBITDA, POS, and so on.

Furthermore, owing to the lightning speed of internet connections, many businesses have questioned the traditional requirement of good office spaces and regimented working hours, because people can now simply Skype or FaceTime or tele-conference others, rather than holding physical meetings that might involve long hours of travel. Soon, businesses might run like the Open University, with discussions and transactions taking place in cyberspace by remote control. Indeed, we can now readily do business in the bathroom with just a towel round our waist, in bed in our pyjamas or naked, or while out walking our dogs. We can now live far away from our business headquarters; as long as we have a good WiFi connection, we could be in the middle of the wilderness, thousands of miles away. Very soon, there will be internet on all commercial airlines and our lives will constantly be further interrupted by business. Whether such increased efficiency in communication will enhance the business world or not remains to be seen. All that is certain is that all of these novelties have presented us with a whole host of previously unimaginable social quandaries – just what is the correct form in this brave new world of business?

DRESSING TO IMPRESS

How many suits and pairs of shoes should the 'modern man' have to make a strong, everlasting impression and

improve career prospects in a highly competitive banking environment?

If I were young again and needed a minimum wardrobe to give the best impression, I would have the following: two suits, one dark charcoal grey, one a slightly lighter charcoal grey; two shirts, one blue and one striped; one black-and-dark-blue tie; one white silk or cotton pocket handkerchief; two pairs of black socks; one pair of black laced-up shoes; and one shoe-polishing kit. The last item is essential because you must polish your shoes every day and try to make them spit-shine. A gentleman always wears highly polished shoes. And, of course, black socks, not fancy coloured ones favoured by second-rate comedians or Sloane Rangers.

The suits must not be black because black is common and worn by salesmen in upmarket clothing shops and waiters in trendy restaurants. Just as white shirts are also common. At times, you should interchange the jacket and trousers of the two suits, so that one is not wearing a complete suit, but nearly a suit. This will make one look sophisticated because there is subtlety in wearing an unmatching jacket and trousers. It also suggests a sense of modesty at not being able to afford a complete suit. Don't, however, forget the white handkerchief in the pocket, which shows a sense of detail. And always wear a tie to show respect to whomever you are meeting. That's it: your total kit for banking survival.

David Tang is making several mistakes in his wardrobe advice for a young man. For starters, grey suits are great, but the collection should have at least one dark navy blue suit as well; if one must impress, they can look more serious, and work better with some skin tones. Shoes should be black for sure, but one pair? A good leather shoe needs to breathe and rest; at least two pairs, to be worn on alternate

days. As for black socks, that is quite a faux pas if the shoes are black, not to mention a crime to the shoe, which one assumes is excellent quality and should be seen clearly; perhaps a pair of socks in a solid colour more suitable to the suit trousers. And white shirts may be 'common', whatever that means for Mr Tang, but are de rigueur for eveningwear; so at least one should be in the collection.

First of all, I was giving advice on a 'minimal' wardrobe for the benefit of an impecunious young man who wished to appear worldly. So, immediately, your advice to have two pair of shoes is off the mark. Besides, since when do shoes need to 'breathe'? I thought I had heard enough pretentious descriptions like 'bouquet' from wine buffs, and now it seems I have to suffer 'breathing' shoes from a shoe buff like yourself? What a load of cobblers! On the contrary, a good pair of shoes requires constant wearing, so that they develop proper creases and a sense of maturity. Just observe the shoes of, say, the Prince of Wales, or any decent duke, and you will see evidence of this.

Your suggestion of wearing non-black socks to show off your shoes is also a little contrived. Subtlety is what is required for an interview in the financial services industry. Coloured socks suggest a transient yuppie or a clever-dick like Nick Leeson, neither of which are desirable. Concerning white shirts, the problem is that waiters and salesmen wear them, so our aspiring young man would need a different shade if he wished to stand out. And you think navy blue suits are better for skin tones? Which? White, brown, black or freckled? I fear your proposed substitutions would diminish the chances of our boy getting on in society. I suspect John Betjeman had you in mind.

How should one dress for a job interview? What hints are there for creating a good impression in order to get the job?

The first common-sense rule is never be late for the appointment. The second is to dress appropriately, and never underdress. Men should always wear a jacket and tie. But never a spanking new suit or tie. One ought to look tidy, but the clothes ought to be somewhat worn. Never put on anything fancy, unless you are auditioning to be a clown. For women, I always think a plain white blouse and creased trousers are best. And never wear too much scent or make-up. This is uppermost in my mind at the moment because I have been on 14 long-haul flights from Hong Kong to London to Hong Kong in the past seven weeks. That's 100,000 miles, and I had to cover my nostrils whenever a stewardess approached because of her overpowering perfume. Noticeable make-up merely suggests vanity and camouflage. Men on the whole do not like heavy-duty scent or make-up, especially at work, and so, if your interviewer is male, he will take a dim view of strong perfume or warpaint.

When you enter the room, approach with calmness and a slight smile and only extend your own hand to shake if the interviewer does the same. Otherwise stand until told to sit down. These small gestures are important and will be noticed.

The most important thing for any interviewee is not how you appear but what you know about the person or company offering you the job. Homework, homework and homework is essential beforehand. Anyone can go into a room and offer dedication, hard work and claim to be 'good with people' and that they 'won't let you down'. These are qualities that the interviewer will have taken for granted that you possess. What they want to know is how you think you can contribute to the job. You should make one or two specific suggestions, but ensure they are not stupid ones. Be polite throughout and never raise your voice, and listen carefully before you talk. Never brag or tell a joke. When you leave, it doesn't hurt to make the slightest nod to show respect. The interviewer wants to feel important and superior. And it's your job to make this happen.

I just moved from Hong Kong to boiling Singapore a couple of weeks ago. I like dressing up when going to the office but it seems that this is not customary here. Personal comfort and practicality is preferred to dapperness, at least for men. Should I stick to a certain standard of elegance with tie and jacket or should I just forfeit and blend in with the crowd?

Singapore is the cradle of climatic tedium, of boiling temperature and dripping humidity. But the worst is the freezing conditions of the interiors created by all the air-conditioners that drone on like a chorus of fishwives. So if you live on that island, you oscillate between two extreme temperate zones. The only thing I can suggest is that, every morning, you should first think about whether you are going to spend more time in or out. If in, then wear a suit and a tie. But if you are out most of the time, it might be more suitable for you to put on a pair of Speedos or a Borat mankini.

NETWORKING

I am a shameless brown noser and a social climber extra-ordinaire. Whenever I meet anyone important, my mind starts up like a computer: 'How can this person be useful to me or my business? What can I get out of befriending this person?' I often cancel invitations I have RSVPed to 'ordinary' friends if a better invitation comes along. I also notice I tend to treat rich, famous or powerful people in a more endearing way than I do poor, unknown or ordinary folks. Please tell me my behaviour is kosher in today's materialistic and celebrity-obsessed world. In fact, isn't it almost necessary to adopt this attitude if one is to survive and prosper in our tough, competitive business world?

How naive you are to think that you can succeed in your social mountaineering from just catching the coat-tails of important people at those ghastly receptions at which people constantly look over others' shoulders. Remember the famous story of F. E. Smith whom a scallywag wanted to befriend. He contrived to engage in conversation with his lordship by asking him where the lavatory was. Birkenhead, spotting this, put his arm round the chap's shoulder and said, 'My dear fellow, go down that corridor and you will see a door on your right on which is written the word "Gentlemen". Don't let that deter you!' Remember Kipling's 'If'; ergo, don't lose your common touch!

What are your thoughts about people going round dishing out their name on business cards to those they have just met, typically at a cocktail reception?

The whole business of dispensing name cards at cocktail receptions is pretty infra dig. Some people even put their faces on the cards while others feel the need to register everything with which they are involved and present a folding card with a long list of companies and institutions, one being more meaningless than the next. What makes me laugh most, however, is when I see ambitious networkers palming off their cards to someone like the Prince of Wales or, as I once witnessed, the Queen. What, pray, is the point of that? I once had a dawn meeting with Fidel Castro after which he gave me a box of cigars with his name card attached. The card confirmed that he was the President of Cuba. Come to think of it, it was a modest gesture on his part not to expect people to know who he was, and so it was a rather smooth thing for him to have done.

A correspondent has challenged my chagrin over the handing out of name cards at receptions, accusing me of 'dripping in the old world of snobbery', a world I 'desperately want to be identified and associated with'. Apparently, networkers have the right and should positively be encouraged to get to know people whom they do not know.

What an idiotic charge. First, as someone born and brought up under British colonial rule and bunged into an English boarding school at 13 not speaking any English, I was more at the receiving end of snobbery rather than a practitioner of it.

Second, has the commentator no consideration for those at a reception who find it tiresome to be waylaid by strangers trying to tell them business and other ideas? Maybe at tedious conferences or academic forums, but hardly on social occasions when everyone should have the right to enjoy themselves without being accosted by pushy networkers desperate to tell you what they are doing and how they could be helped. It is also sheer naivety to expect any result with the unilateral offer of cards, or even the exchange of cards. Relationships are not ignited that way. If you really want the proper attention of someone else, you can only get it by making yourself interesting enough for that person to take an interest in you. Merely palming off your name card is almost an insult to the concept of being interesting.

TRICKY SITUATIONS

Recently a friend returned from a business trip in Hong Kong. Invited by a respected Chinese chief executive to the Mandarin spa, he showed up for an afternoon of luxury and was most surprised to find the man dressed in a robe, ready to discuss business. As the meeting unfolded by the pool, my friend could think of one thing only: how to look professional in a bath towel. In order to avoid this

embarrassing situation, how should one conduct business wearing nothing but spa attire?

Only the triads transact serious business in towels. Maybe also the tattooed mafia, or the fingerless yakuza. But no self-respecting Chinese chief executive would dream of having a business meeting in semi-nakedness. So your friend must be dealing with a very questionable Chinaman.

He would be well advised to beat a hasty retreat by feigning conjunctivitis or psoriasis. But if he had dithered and was already in spa attire, then the only professional thing to do would have been to carry on regardless, totally ignoring the bizarre surroundings. That's exactly what a pro does: he gets on with it.

As a consultant who travels frequently for business, my clients recommend hotels that are near their offices and which meet their budgets. The hotels provide the basics but they do not compensate for the rigours of the road and their airstrip isolation can preclude the benefits of networking in town. Is it poor form to bill clients for the rate from the hotel they recommended, and pay the difference for a better one out of my pocket to stay at the hotel of my choice?

If your clients regard their choice of accommodation as good enough for you, then that is the measure of your 'grade'. Therefore, if you think you deserve better, then either your clients underestimate your value or you yourself overestimate your own. Either of these suggests that you should not try to upgrade your assigned accommodation. Much better for you to work harder and become cleverer so that your clients become unequivocally dependent on you and put you in a hotel of your choice. Your status is worth much more when it is recognized by people who pay you commensurate with what you do.

My employer appears to have forgotten to give me a bonus this year – how best to broach this subject?

You must of course find out if your privation was due to a deliberate intention or simple inadvertence on the part of your boss. A subtle way might be to ask him if he wanted to sit down to do the annual bonuses for EVERYONE in the office. Or more subtly, you can, at the right moment of pausing while you are taking his dictation or notes, drop in a couple of place names, like the South Sea islands, mentioning that you have always wanted to visit them, and then pausing yourself to say something like: 'Of course, I would only be able to do that if I saved up from a couple of years' bonuses.' At that precise moment, you must look your boss straight in the eye, and adjudge if he was just mean or amnesiac.

My employer leads a very high-profile business life and has recently been in the press rather a lot. I am finding it exhausting and humiliating that wherever I go, I am seemingly defined by, 'Oh, do meet . . . she works for . . .' I am always having to preface everything with a rather chippy-sounding, 'Yes, well, I am a person in my own right with a life full of interest and intellectual pursuits outside of my work life.' How can I live a life uncluttered by being merely a vessel for my employer's already burgeoning ego?

You are obviously not a very loyal employee. Generally, you will be frowned upon, and in a country like Japan you would be ostracized. Indeed, you seem almost certainly to be court-martial material if you were to be in the army. The trouble is that nowadays, there is scarcely any sense of subordination, duty or loyalty. It is character-building to admit to something that you don't quite agree with and show a sense of reverence to authority. That indeed had been the Confucian system in China for 2,500 years until the Communist Party smashed it up.

On yet another business trip with my boss I found myself subjected to yet another evening of his useless and excruciatingly stupid/boring conversations cum lectures. I am going to kill myself if I have to endure any more. Seriously, any advice on how to suffer fools gladly? My work is otherwise pleasant.

I suppose if you were to kill yourself that would indeed solve the problem. But for something less drastic you might, when your boss is holding forth, choose to be totally silent and just nod your head or, if you are Indian, shake it from side to side. Sooner or later he will realize that your reticent obsequiousness is irritating and he might even dry up. Recently in Madrid I sat next to a rather tiresome woman who said to me: 'Now, David, I have not seen you for three years. Tell me what you have been doing.' My reply to her was: 'I have done nothing in the last three years. Why don't you tell me what you have been doing in the last three years, and I will eat?'

I am a deferential but ambitious young employee at a large Asian company and over the festive season, in keeping with Chinese traditions, my boss sent me an elaborate gift set of preserved meats. Unfortunately I am a philo-Semite and the stench of Chinese sausage has offended my strictly kosher

sensibilities. I am in a real pickle as I do not wish to seem rude nor damage my long-term career prospects. What is the correct etiquette in this predicament?

In a nutshell, you want to know how you can suck up to your boss when he has given you something you cannot enjoy. To protest would make you seem disrespectful and ungrateful; whereas to feign gratitude and enjoyment would make you a liar. My advice for such corporate pole-vaulting is to be practical with Machiavellian cunning. If your boss is egotistical and loves to be flattered, then you should simply say: 'Thank you for your thoughtfulness.' But if your boss is civilized and forthright, then you should confess that what he has given you goes against your religion. An understanding boss will respect you for it. In other words, forget about veracity and etiquette. Concentrate on how to maximize the brownie points you would get from your boss. Meanwhile, pass on your preserved meat to someone who is not kosher, and make use of what you don't need as the pretension of generosity.

The other day I was in a meeting with a (as you would say) *grand fromage* from my company. Rather than paying any interest to his colleagues or the matter being discussed he seemed more interested in checking, in turn, each of the three electronic devices laid in front of him. To be fair, he did occasionally bark a vaguely relevant comment. What are your thoughts on such behaviour and how should a measly underling respond?

You are lucky. My great friend the Duchess of York has six devices all sheathed in different colours and flashes and sounds. I usually need a Van de Graaff generator jammer before I can catch her concentration. For you, why don't you try texting your *grand fromage* while you are in the meeting?

You could text him 'Cheese!' I have to say that not only in meetings, but in all conceivable spaces – restaurants, lobbies, lifts, cars, buses, trains, planes, cinemas and even public lavatories – everybody is gazing into their iPhones and BlackBerrys. It has become the fastest-growing disease of our time.

When is it too late for a work colleague to telephone one at night – I think 10.45pm is de trop?

The measure of a good relationship is precisely how late one could ring the other. But nowadays texting or emailing on mobile devices is much less intrusive than calling, and timing becomes less of a deciding factor. There is, of course, WhatsApp, which offers voice exchanges and is, I gather, very popular among the young. Certainly in China its equivalent WeChat is exceedingly popular among both the young and the fossils. Maybe it's because it's much more convenient and faster to speak than write out all the characters in Chinese.

I have recently been awarded an honour for political services. I am told I can now apply to the College of Arms for a coat of arms. The King of Arms says this must include allusions and references to my life and achievements. My entire career has been in mergers and acquisitions, some of which worked and others which didn't. What do you suggest?

In modern life, when will you use your coat of arms? On your signet ring? A bit Sloaney, don't you think? For a seal in wax? 'Shurely shome mishtake!' When you are a banker-turned-politician, I should keep piano about your honour, as there is a presumption of greed among bankers and disingenuousness among politicians. You will more likely become a symbol of contempt than admiration. Besides, it costs £8,000 to register a new coat of arms. That in itself should be sufficient reason for someone who is proud of their honour not to spend such an exorbitant sum to flaunt it.